clock book

recipes from a modern Moroccan kitchen

by Tara Stevens

with photographs by Julius Honnor

boo33ks.

Published in 2010 by 33books ltd
33books ltd is a company registered in England, no. 7069485

Text © Tara Stevens 2010
Photographs © Julius Honnor 2010,
except those pp16, 23, 30, 64, 77–9, 124 and 138–9, which © Tara Stevens 2010

Printed on 100% recycled paper in Great Britain by ArtQuarters Press, East London.

A CIP data record is available for this book from the British Library.
ISBN 978-0-9566600-0-8

contents

foreword

My earliest memories are tinged with the scent of Moroccan cuisine.

I was born in England and subjected to a childhood of grey school uniforms, even greyer skies, and to food so bland that it tasted of almost nothing at all. But, unlike my friends in the playground, I was certain the real world was out there – somewhere. It was a fantasy, a Promised Land, a realm of rich textures and dazzling light, a place where the air was fragrant with spices, and the kitchens abundant with the most magical ingredients.

This secret knowledge came about because of my family's love affair for Morocco. My first journeys there were made as a small child in the early '70s – a time when the kingdom was awash with stoned hippies and tie-dye, VW Combis and Rolling Stones songs. I didn't quite understand how a place could be so different from the world in which I lived. It was so utterly mesmerising, vibrant and so culturally colourful.

I can remember the pungent, intoxicating scent of orange blossom on Tangier's rue de la Plage in spring, and the taste of summer melons in Marrakech. My tongue still tingles at the thought of the warm almond pastry passed to me one balmy September afternoon in Chefchaoen. And, as for my first sugar-sprinkled *b'stilla* – it stole my heart.

Then decades passed.

My feet traipsed through forgotten corners of the world, but never found their way back to my first true love – Morocco. Sometimes on my journeys I would close my eyes and be transported back as if in a dream – to the windswept sea wall of Essaouira, or to Marrakech's Jma al Fna square, or to the twisting, labyrinthine streets of medieval Fez. I would breathe in deeply and sigh, feasting on the smells and the memories.

Then, one morning, living in an East End flat no bigger than a postage stamp, I had a Eureka moment. It was so obvious. We would embrace the land of my fantasy: we'd go and live in Morocco.

And we did.

It was like stepping through a keyhole into a world touched by a magician's wand. In the six years we have lived here, we have glimpsed an unbroken circle of life that's been eroded and disjointed elsewhere. It's a world dominated by values – by chivalry and honesty, by charity and, above all, by a sense of family.

And at the same time, it's a world dominated by food.

Anyone who has ever spent time in Morocco has been charmed from the first meal by the kingdom's astonishing range of dishes. Through succulent flavours, textures, ingredients, and through sheer artistry – they go together to form an ancient kind of alchemy all of their own.

One of the first things I learned while living here is that most Moroccans prefer eating their own cuisine at home. A meal, especially one prepared for guests, is a sumptuous blend of hospitality and abundance, and is about honouring the invited as much as it is about feeding them. The dishes presented tend to be enjoyed communally, eaten from a central platter or tajine. And, of course, each home has its own carefully guarded recipes, passed on through centuries from mother to daughter.

Like most of my Moroccan friends, I too am sometimes reluctant to eat in restaurants. As with them, I know that what we have at home is superior to almost anything found outside.

But there are exceptions.

When I first heard that an Englishman had given up a promising culinary career in London's West End, swapping it for the Fez medina – where he planned to start afresh – I rolled my eyes. Then I put my head in my hands. It sounded like a recipe for catastrophe.

But stepping across the threshold of the Café Clock, I was utterly mesmerised. Not only was its founder, Mike Richardson, a man of magnetic charm, but he had conjured a spellbinding ambience in the heart of a city I hold so dear.

And, as for the food… Far too canny to try (and fail) to recreate Moroccan home cooking in a restaurant like so many before him, instead Mike created a menu of café food inspired by the myriad flavours of the medina – truly Moroccan and truly modern.

Café Clock's success lies in the subtle flavours of a culinary tradition which itself stands at a crossroads of geography and culture. It is made possible by seasonal foods, by spices and by raw ingredients that have found their way to the medieval city through centuries, along the pilgrimage routes. After all, for more than a thousand years, Fez has been connected to the farthest reaches of the Islamic world, to destinations as varied as Seville, Cairo, Timbuktu, Bokhara, Kabul and Samarkand.

With time, Café Clock has become far more than a place to dine well. In the tradition of the ancient caravanserais, once found in every town and city between it and Mecca and beyond, it's a place where people gather. Some are locals, while many more are travellers, gorging themselves on the intensity of Fez for the first time. Together, they swap stories, talk, listen, laugh, and learn from the endless range of cultural events laid on in the crucible that is Café Clock.

Just as I had been anxious at hearing of an Englishman opening a restaurant in Fez, I had wondered a little anxiously how the *Clock Book* might look. Making the shift from the experimental fluidity of a kitchen, to the restricted world of the printed page is not easy. It's a realm in which too many talented food writers have failed.

But what strikes me squarely between the eyes is how the author, Tara Stevens, has approached this project. From the outset she's harnessed an astonishing perspicacity and a clear sense of observation. Through watching, tasting and, above all, through listening, she has brought to this book's pages a rare and comprehensive culinary experience.

At the same time, Tara has explained how and where specific ingredients are sourced, and has clarified the ways in which they are used in the kitchens of Café Clock.

The result is far more than a cookbook. It's a key. Immerse yourself in its pages and, in return, it will unlock a domain that's more usually cloaked in mystery, and quite off limits to the outside world. Study the pages well, and the ancient alchemy is revealed.

Tahir Shah
Casablanca, 2010

تفهمى

مكة المكرمة

introduction

Arriving in the old medina of Fez for the first time is much like stepping back in time. By about 1000 years. Once you cross the threshold of the Bab Boujloud a whole new universe unfolds. Live chickens cluck from behind the doors of their wire cages before a customer looking for the contents of a tagine seals their fate. Next door a man skins rabbits, and offers hedgehogs as a key ingredient for a fabled soup to cure head colds. Farmers down from the middle Atlas sell plump white mulberries one week, and *arbuces* – a soft red berry fruit the colour of garnets – the next; baskets of spiky wild artichokes and rose petals from the Dades Valley jostle up against barrows filled with eggs and heaps of hand-rolled couscous. Modern supermarkets suddenly seem very far away. And all this takes place to a daily theatre of folk dressed in djellabas and Gnawa musicians spinning their heads and rattling tin *krakab* (a forerunner to the Spanish castanet), all woven between the ancient and mysterious sounding calls to prayer of the muezzin. Here is a place where people still believe in magic and that, inshallah, whatever happens will happen because that is the way it is meant to be. So when people tell you that in Morocco you don't find a house, it finds you, it rings completely true.

Mike Richardson had come from a successful career as maître d' at the Wolseley, one of London's top restaurants, and wanted a life change. A friend of his had suggested Fez, and Mike quickly found himself aboard a plane with £20,000 in his pocket, determined to create something new. Little did he know at the time that what he would end up creating would become one of the most important social centres in the city, a true hub for Moroccans, expats and people passing through. Today, Fez without the Café Clock is unthinkable.

This being Morocco, the process was fraught with unpredictable twists and turns. The first house he put a deposit on fell though, meaning the deposit returned to him doubled. It also meant there would be no backing out. In Morocco the law dictates that the money has to stay there or be reinvested in something else, which left him with two choices: either become a carpet salesman back in London, or find something else fast. With the money safely hidden in a suitcase under the bed of a friend he did what any Moroccan would do – put his faith in God and assumed a solution would be forthcoming.

Days later he received an email containing snapshots of a dilapidated house in the middle of the Fez medina. Peering closely at the wreckage he caught glimpses of the ancient *zellij* and the carefully crafted wrought iron details of the balconies, and he bought it. 'I wasn't totally sure what I was doing or where I was going with it,' Mike explains. 'But I felt that Fez needed something different: a pizzeria, a French bistro, maybe. Eventually I decided on a café because I wanted to include a cultural element, and I wanted it to feel alive all day, not just for the lunch or dinner. I also wanted to do something that was true to the country, something that celebrated Morocco's great culinary heritage, but was fresh and modern, which was how the famed camel burger came about.

'I was in the medina one day with Tariq, my head chef at the time, and passing the camel butchers I found myself wondering what a camel burger would be like. So we bought a half kilo of camel kefta, mixed on the spot by the butcher, and tried making it back at the café. It was so good I thought right, I'm taking all other burgers off the menu: let them eat camel.

'It was about this time, when I'd begun to realise that I might need some help, that Max walked through the door. He'd just moved to Morocco and had owned several successful restaurants in Coffs Harbour, Australia. He was looking for somewhere to live, I needed a flat-mate and someone to bounce ideas off. It wasn't long before I realised he was the right-hand man I'd been looking for and he'd just dropped in my lap. No doubt about it, this place has *baraka*.'

Baraka – the quality of being blessed, serendipity, or plain good luck: Café Clock has it in spades. Following my first visit I began exploring the idea of a book about Moroccan food. Then I got my call: Mike wanted someone to do the *Clock Book*, a collection of modern Moroccan recipes from the café and inspired by the ingredients of the medina.

It was the opportunity I had been looking for. Moroccan cuisine is so much more than the ubiquitous tagines and couscous. Rather, it is a complex weaving together of the fundamental tastes of sweet and salt, bitter and aromatic, always seeking balance and harmony so that one taste does not overpower any other. It is rich in exotic spices like cinammon, cardamom and cumin, and in fragrant herbs like mint, coriander and *shiba* (*Artemisia absinthium*: absinthe herb or more commonly wormwood), which is slipped into tea in winter to keep the chill from your bones; and like all cuisines it is one that is continually evolving.

This is my record of the dishes and the stories I have encountered in more than a year of regular visits to the Fez medina. I have worked closely with Mike and Max and their cooks Tariq and Souad to come up with something that I hope is authentic and will give readers a taste of what it is to inhabit this world, so close geographically and yet so different from our own.

Together, we have updated many of the traditional dishes of Morocco to bring them more in line with 21st-century lifestyles, which means we account for busy working weeks as well as healthier diets and the Western kitchen, where modern isn't necessarily the best: once you've eaten bread baked in the public *ferran* (wood-fired oven) our own westernised version seems bland and unexciting.

At the Clock most of the daily specials are dictated by the seasons, and though I've included the recipes here you won't always find them on the menu. Likewise, in the case of some of the more unusual ingredients used – such as camel meat or desert truffles – I've suggested alternatives that can easily be found back home.

And although this book is largely a taste of the Café Clock, I was also keen to highlight some of the less well-known yet truly great dishes of the land. Morocco has no big tradition of restaurant dining – the finest feasts are always eaten in somebody's home – but if you dig deep, it is there to be discovered. If the Café Clock has taught me anything at all, it is that we have the most remarkable cuisine right here in the heart of our beloved medina: a true taste of modern Morocco.

Tara Stevens

breakfast
and brunch

The Fez medina can seem like one huge market: a living and breathing larder. You can find anything and everything here if you know where to look, and buying it is all part of the fun.

The day starts comparatively late at the Clock, with the first customers generally sauntering through the door at about the same time that the *khobz* (bread) comes back from the *ferran* (the communal cooking fires to be found in every district) at around 9 am.

But if you're an early bird, you can't beat a bowl of *b'sarra* – broad bean or split pea soup traditionally eaten for breakfast in Morocco – from a hole-in-the-wall café in the medina, which opens around 8 am and shuts as soon as the last bowl of soup has been served.

Breakfast b'sarra (serves 4) (V)

B'sarra is one of the easiest soups in the world to make, but isn't made at the Clock since one of the great treats of the medina is to eat on the street. I usually get it at a stall near the Bab Boujloud for breakfast. A small bowl will cost you about 6 dirhams (50 pence) and sets you up for the day nicely. Don't just save it for breakfast though: served with plenty of crusty bread, it's exactly the kind of dish that keeps you going at night through the long northern European winter.

400 g split peas, soaked overnight
6 cloves garlic, thinly sliced
1 large mild onion, sliced
2 tsp ground cumin
2 tsp sweet paprika
2 tsp rose-infused salt
Approx 2 litres water
2–3 tbsp argan or olive oil
salt and pepper

1   Sauté the garlic and onion in olive oil until translucent and aromatic, but not coloured

2   Add the peas, spices and salt

3   Cover in water to just over an inch above the peas

4   Bring to a boil then simmer until the peas are tender (about 1 hour), adding more water if it begins to look dry

5   Puree with a hand-blender and return to the pan

6   Add more water if needed, check for seasoning

7   Serve with a small bowl of freshly ground cumin and another of harissa (or three parts paprika to one part cayenne) to sprinkle on top of the soup, wedges of fresh lemon, a swirl of argan or olive oil, and plenty of fresh *khobz* (see p134)

Variation

Add less water at stage 4 and you end up with a thick puree that when cool can be used as a dip. Dress it with a sprinkle of cumin and harissa, and a drizzle of argan oil before serving.

Clock-a-doodle doo – a breakfast of champions (V)

The selection of dried fruit and nuts in the medina is so vast that the concept of boring old muesli has taken on a whole new meaning for me. The Clock toasts French oats in-house under the watchful eye of Souad to make sure they don't burn, then she adds whatever looks good: chopped medjool dates (a plump and very sweet Middle Eastern variety), figs, sultanas, dried cranberries, almonds, hazelnuts, pistachios, and sprinkled with a little ground cardamom and cinnamon to spice it up. This is what I call the 'full monty' version, which makes about half a kilo of muesli that you can store in an airtight container for weeks. Clock serves it with a generous dollop of Fatima's home-made goat's milk yogurt and a drizzle of lavender honey from the souks.

250 g coarse porridge oats
50 g almonds
50 g hazelnuts
50 g pistachio nuts
50 g dates
50 g dried figs
50 g sultanas
50 g dried cranberries
2 tsp ground cinnamon
2 tsp ground cardamom

1　Preheat the oven to 160°C

2　Spread the oats over a baking tray and bake on the middle rack for 10 minutes, stirring once or twice to prevent them from burning

3　Chop the fruit and nuts into small dice and mix together

4　Sprinkle on the spices, stir well to combine with other ingredients and store in an air-tight container

5　Serve with milk, a dollop of Greek yogurt and a drizzle of runny honey

Attention à la tête

Mind your head

**Clock fuel – the ultimate energy bar
(makes 8 bars) (V)**

This dish was inspired by *majoun*, the legendary psychoactive sweetmeat made with cannabis and used by Sufi orders to open the mind. More traditionally, and without the cannabis, this is the kind of food, known as *smita*, that is given to women just before and after childbirth. Dates in particular are known to enrich mother's milk and provide an additional boost to newborns. I always take them on research trips as you never know what might happen on the road, but you can rely on these keeping you going from dawn until dusk.

50 g dates
50 g dried figs
50 g dried apricots
50 g almonds, skinless
50 g hazelnuts, skinless
2 tbsp white sesame seeds
2 tbsp honey
Juice of 1 lemon
1 tsp ground cinnamon
8 sheets warka or filo pastry
1 egg, beaten

1   Steam the dates and the figs for 5 minutes to soften and bring out the flavours

2   Finely chop all of the fruit, and pound the nuts (not the sesame seeds) in a pestle and mortar to get a coarse crumb

3   Mix the fruit and nuts together in a pan over a low heat

4   Add the sesame seeds, honey, lemon and cinnamon, stir for 1 minute and remove from the heat

5   Knead the mixture together with your hands until you get a soft 'dough'

6   Using 2 sheets of pastry per sausage, wrap the pastry around the dough to form 4 'sausage rolls'

7   Glaze with beaten egg and bake in the oven at 200°C for 10 minutes or until golden

8   Cool on a wire rack. These will keep in an airtight container for several days

Khlee baked eggs (serves 4)

Khlee is often described as beef jerky, but to my mind it is more like a confit. The meat – usually beef or mutton – is cured in salt, coriander and garlic, semi-dried and covered in rendered beef or sheep fat, after which it will last indefinitely. Once removed from the fat, the meat is butter-tender and mellow in flavour. This is an unusual and very special brunch dish that's perfect winter's day material.

1   Sauté the onions and garlic in oil in a shallow pan over a low heat for 10 minutes until golden

2   Add half the tomatoes and cook for a further 15 minutes until really caramelised

3   Add the *khlee* and its fat, if using, and cook for 5 minutes

4   Add the spices, salt and a good pinch of black pepper, cover, turn the heat down low and cook for 10 minutes, check for seasoning

5   Preheat the oven to 240° and heat a tagine or oven-proof serving dish for 10 minutes

6   Add the tomatoes and the peppers to the *khlee* or bacon mix, take off the heat and turn the oven down to 200°

7   Add two tbsp tomato and *khlee* mix to the dish, break in an egg, cover and transfer to the oven for 7–9 minutes (soft baked) or until just set

8   Sprinkle the yolk with freshly ground cumin and herbs, and serve straight from the dish, warm with flatbreads

2 onions, halved and thinly sliced

4 garlic cloves, halved lengthways

6 roasted green peppers, peeled and cut into strips about ½ cm wide

4 large tomatoes – peel, cut in half, scoop out the seeds, cut into eighths

100 g khlee or slices of cooked beef or left-over duck (bacon is also a good substitute), shredded (or cut into thin strips if using bacon)

1 tbsp khlee fat or butter (optional)

1 tbsp roughly chopped parsley

1 tbsp roughly chopped coriander

4 eggs

1 tbsp olive oil

1 tsp cumin

1 tsp paprika

salt and pepper

Moroccan crumpets with fresh cheese and dried fruit confit (serves 4) (V)

Medina street food is one of the great delights of Fez and you'll notice lots of stalls, especially near the Bab Boujloud, selling a variety of breads and pastries. One of these is a giant Moroccan crumpet called *beghreer*, puffed up and pocked with tiny holes much like the English version. Clock does a smaller version of them and usually serves them with caramelised bananas.

1   Combine the flours, yeast, baking powder and salt in a bowl, pour a small amount of water over the top and leave for 2–3 minutes to activate the yeast

2   Add the rest of the water and whisk well (or pop it in a blender) until you have a smooth batter, cover with a tea towel and leave in a warm place to prove for 30 minutes

3   Heat a non-stick frying pan over a high heat until smoking hot

4   Pour in one ladleful of batter at a time. As soon as the top starts to pock and set, flip the pancake to brown the uncooked side

5   Cook for another minute and turn on to a serving platter; stack, cover in foil and keep warm in a low oven

6   Top with mascarpone cheese and the fruit confit

For the confit

1   Combine the orange and lemon juices, honey, cardamom and butter and bring to a boil

2   As soon as the juices are boiling add the dried fruit and keep on a rolling heat to reduce the liquid but retain the firmness of the fruit

3   Once all of the liquid has evaporated stir in the cinnamon and the orange flower essence

Batter mix

250 g fine semolina flour
125 g plain white flour
1 tsp salt
2 tsp (18 g) dried yeast
1 sachet (7 g) baking powder
600 ml warm water

Dried fruit confit

8 prunes, diced
10 dried apricots, diced
6 dried figs, diced
200 ml orange juice
juice of 1 lemon
4 tbsp honey
2 cardamom pods, split open to reveal the seeds
1 tbsp butter
pinch of ground cinammon
2 tsp orange flower essence

To serve

4 tbsp mascarpone or curd cheese

Variations

These crumpets work well with both sweet and savoury toppings. Try them with hot with butter and honey, caramelised bananas and Greek yogurt; cream cheese, smoked salmon and a dollop of caviar, or even with just with a drizzle of olive oil. Yummy.

Scrambled eggs with desert truffles (serves 4) (V)

Although it looks very similar to European truffles the desert truffle is quite different in taste. The texture is moist and tender with the flavour of extremely fresh hazelnuts or almond milk. They are very mild, and if you can find them fresh (in Morocco May–June) when they are gathered from the arid Sub-Sahara and transported up to Fez they are something remarkable.

Like all truffles, they lend themselves particularly well to eggs and cream sauces and they've become a Clock signature breakfast during the annual Fez World Sacred Music Festival.

2 tbsp large knob butter

8 fresh eggs

100 ml cream

1 tsp paprika

2 khobz (see p134) split in half longways and toasted

1 small desert truffle (substitute black or white truffles, or a drizzle of truffle oil)

salt and pepper

1   Melt the butter in a pan over a gentle heat

2   Whisk the eggs gently so that they are broken rather than foamy

3   Pour the eggs over the butter and stir in the cream, paprika, salt and pepper

4   Toast the bread while the eggs cook

5   Spoon the eggs over the bread (one half *khobz* per person)

6   Shave over a generous heap of truffle

7   Serve immediately

Koolshi kedgeree (serves 4)

This isn't technically a Clock dish, but makes good use of any leftover couscous you might have from other Clock recipes. *Koolshi* means 'everything' and just about sums up this Moroccan-style kedgeree. I've used salmon (frozen fish is fine for this dish), but you could also do it with ready-smoked mackerel. Don't be put off by the long list of ingredients: putting it together is a cinch.

To cook the salmon

1 In a frying pan, add 1 cm water plus the bay leaves, a pinch of salt and freshly ground pepper; bring to the boil

2 Add the salmon fillets, skin side down

3 Simmer gently until the flesh has turned pale pink

4 Remove the salmon from the pan, and place flesh side up on a plate to cool

To boil the eggs

1 Place the eggs in a pan of cold water, bring to the boil and simmer for 2 minutes

2 Remove from the heat, cover and leave to sit in the hot water for 5 minutes (for a soft yolk)

3 Remove the eggs, crack the shell and rinse under cold water to stop the cooking process, peel

4 Split into quarters just before serving

To make the dressing

1 Combine the crème fraîche, coriander and chillies, set aside to let the flavours develop

To make the kedgeree

1 Melt the butter and olive oil together over a medium heat, fry the onion and garlic until soft and golden

2 Add the ginger and ras al hanout, stir for 2–3 minutes to release the flavours

3 Add the couscous and tomatoes, gently toss to combine all the ingredients, check for seasoning

4 Remove the skin from the salmon (it will come away easily), flake and gently toss with the couscous

5 Arrange the quartered eggs on top

6 Serve with the crème fraîche mixed dressing

---

2 salmon fillets (or mackerel)

2 bay leaves

2 eggs

1 large white onion, finely chopped

3 cloves garlic, thinly sliced

2 tbsp (about 3 thumbs) ginger, freshly grated

2 tbsp ras al hanout (substitute garam masala if desired)

8 baby plum tomatoes, quartered (plus any leftover vegetables you might have, cut to the same size)

8 heaped tbsp leftover couscous (substitute leftover rice if desired)

1 tbsp olive oil

1 tbsp butter

4 lemon quarters

salt and pepper

For the dressing

1 small tub crème fraîche

2 tbsp fresh coriander, chopped

2 hot green chillies, sliced

burgers
and sandwiches

Nothing epitomises the notion of café food like a big, fat, juicy burger or a monstrous sandwich spilling out at the seams. The Clock has got these down to a fine art, changing the contents of each according to the season.

But if ever there was a dish that could be credited with making a place famous it has to be the camel burger. For me it's not only something I associate with the Clock, but a tribute to the culinary heritage of North Africa, the Sahara and the Middle East.

The history books say that the first-ever burger in a bun was invented in 1905 at Delmonico's, New York City. But if we're talking the first ever 'burger patty', that can be traced back to Genghis Khan's invasion of the Middle East in the 11th century, when he and his fierce Mongol warriors were known to sit in the saddle for days or even weeks during their rampages without ever dismounting. To sustain themselves, they would slip chunks of meat under the saddle before going into battle. It would emerge pulverised and tender, ready to eat raw once the battle was won.

The street food vendors of the medina have been cooking up their own versions of the Khan burger ever since: a giant, sliced sausage stuffed with liver, a soupçon of fat and handfuls of secret spices that you'll see and smell at the upper ends of Ta'laa K'bira and Ta'laa S'ghira.

The Clock burger combines the exotic flavours of Morocco in a more Western way, and is served in true fast-food style with a side of twice-fried fries, tossed in spicy harissa or aromatic ras al hanout. I'm really happy too that it comes with its very own Taza ketchup. Enjoy.

Camel burger (serves 4)

The camel burger has been a bestseller since day one, especially since the butcher revealed his secret ingredient – dried rose petals from the Dades Valley – that turns the patties into a powerful aphrodisiac. All who eat it, he told me, would be touched by love. Of course, if your local butcher can't get their hands on a juicy piece of camel steak, you could always substitute beef.

1   Put the lot through a food processor on pulse (don't make it too mushy), knead together and shape into 4 patties, cover and chill well before cooking (it helps the meat to bind together)

2   Fry on a dry pan or skillet for 4 minutes either side or to your preferred level of doneness

3   Serve on a toasted sesame bun with Taza ketchup and all the trimmings: a slice of cheese added to the patty just before the end of cooking time, slices of tomato and onion rings

Taza ketchup

1   Blend the tomatoes in a processor until fairly smooth then gently sauté in a little olive oil for 5 minutes

2   Add the cinnamon and sugar, season and simmer until the sauce is thick and glossy (about 10 minutes)

1 kg camel meat, minced
1 tbsp camel hump, or butter (optional)
4 tbsp red onions, chopped
6 garlic cloves, crushed
2 tbsp coriander, chopped
2 tbsp parsley, chopped
2 tbsp mint, chopped
2 tbsp dried rose petals
2 tsp ground cumin
2 tsp red paprika
1 tsp cloves, crushed
juice of lemon
salt and pepper

Taza ketchup
5–6 ripe tomatoes, roughly chopped
4 tsp ground cinnamon
4 tsp honey
olive oil
salt and pepper

Lamb beldi burger (serves 4)

Mike's friend Aimi, who came to Fez to help with the Clock's launch, came up with this – a lighter take on the camel burger

1. Knead together the lamb, cumin, parsley, salt and pepper
2. Add the diced feta cheese, taking care not to break up the chunks
3. Shape into patties and pan fry over a medium heat until the patty is pink and juicy
4. Serve in a plain white bun with thin slices of red onion and a dollop of cucumber and mint salsa

Cucumber and mint salsa

1. Combine all the ingredients together in a bowl, and chill well before serving

1 kg minced lamb
1 tbsp ground cumin
1 tbsp parsley, finely chopped
250 g feta cheese, crumbled into large chunks
salt and pepper

Cucumber and mint salsa

1 cucumber, peeled and finely diced
2 tbsp fresh mint, finely chopped
1–2 green chillies, thinly sliced
3 tbsp plain Greek yogurt
1 tsp sugar

Spiced fried chicken sandwich with red pepper and almond salsa (serves 4)

Tariq's fried chicken sandwich is the quickest way I know of transporting myself back to the souks without getting on a plane. The same marinade also works well for roasting. I also use it on quail and poussins to serve with harissa roast potatoes (see p102).

1. Mix the spices, garlic, lemon juice and oil together and rub into the chicken breasts. Place in a zip-lock or sealed plastic bag and leave to marinate for at least two hours, or overnight in the fridge

2. Bring to room temperature and fry in a splash of olive oil until the outside is crisp and golden, and the middle cooked through (about 5 minutes total)

3. Toast the *khobz* on both sides and spread with butter or mayonnaise. Add a heap of bitter leaves like frisée, slices of cucumber and a dollop of the red pepper and almond salsa

Red pepper and almond salsa

1. Combine all the ingredients in a bowl and chop to a coarse salsa with a hand blender or food processor, or by hand in a pestle and mortar.

2 large chicken breasts, butterfly down the length of the breast to make two thin fillets

2 garlic cloves, crushed

2 tsp cinnamon

2 tsp cumin

1 tbsp lemon juice

1 tbsp oil

4 plain khobz

Red pepper and almond salsa

2 large red peppers

2 cloves garlic, crushed

50 g flaked almonds

1 red chilli, chopped

1 tbsp parsley, chopped

1 tbsp sherry or red wine vinegar

1 tbsp olive oil

1 tsp sea salt

Chickpea, preserved lemon and coriander burger (serves 4) (V)

This is the Clock's version of falafel: rich, moist and fragrant with herbs, it was inspired by a street vendor named Abdul who hawks the most delectable steamed chickpea sandwich from his street cart in r'Cif, at the heart of the medina. If you've made a batch of spiced preserved lemons use them to make this dish. The spice gives it a satisfying kick. If you haven't got any preserved lemons use the zest of one lemon. It's not quite the same, but it works. You can substitute tinned chickpeas elsewhere, but the dried ones hold the burger together much better in this case.

400 g dried chickpeas, soaked overnight and cooked until tender (the effort is worth it for this dish), husks removed

50 g breadcrumbs

½ preserved lemon, flesh removed, skin rinsed and finely chopped

6 garlic cloves, crushed

2 tsp harissa (dry or wet)

3 tbsp fresh coriander, chopped

2 tbsp olive oil

2 tbsp tahini

2 tbsp water

salt and pepper

Sweet green pepper relish

6 green peppers

1 green chilli, chopped (optional)

2 tbsp lemon juice

1 tbsp vegetable oil

3 tsp honey

1   Mix together all the ingredients with a hand blender or food processor and check for seasoning. Aim for chunky rather than smooth. Add a tiny bit more water if the patty mix is too dry, but bear in mind it needs to be fairly dry to hold together

2   Shape into 1 cm thick patties (you'll get about 8 out of this batch) and chill for at least 30 minutes

3   Heat a heavy frying pan so that it's good and hot, turn down to medium, and cook the patties for approx 3 minutes on each side or until golden

4   Serve in a split pitta (see p140) with lettuce, slices of tomato and red onion, and a dollop of sweet green pepper relish and plain yogurt

Sweet green pepper relish

1   Preheat the oven to 200°C and roast the peppers on a baking tray until their skin blackens. If you have a gas stove top, you can also place the peppers on top of the flame, turning once or twice so the skin blackens. Try to retain some crunch

2   Place the blackened peppers into plastic bags and leave to cool, when you remove them the skins will come off easily

3   Whisk together the lemon juice, oil and honey (and chilli, if using)

4   Halve the peppers, remove the seeds and dice finely

5   Toss the peppers with the lemon and honey mix, and chill before serving

Fennel seed khobz with grilled vegetables, goat's cheese and fig and date chutney (serves 4) (V)

Fatima's home-made goat's cheese is one of the great pleasures of living in the medina. Her husband has a small herd of goats that roam from hill to hill in the middle Atlas living on wild herbs, figs and grasses. She sets the cheese in beautiful green, woven baskets that she makes herself and brings into town. The Clock buys both the young, fresh version that Tariq uses in his cheesecake and on pancakes, and a pungent, aged cheese that goes brilliantly with sweet grilled vegetables and chutney.

Back home the classic French goat's log is a good substitute or you could use something like haloumi. I like to use khobz with fennel seeds for this sandwich, which goes well with the sourness of the cheese.

250 g goat's cheese, cut into slices
1 aubergine, sliced lengthwise
1 red pepper, sliced lengthwise
1 courgette, sliced lengthwise
3 tbsp olive oil
1 tbsp balsamic vinegar
1 tsp dried oregano
salt and pepper
4 fennel seed khobz

1   Toss the aubergine, red pepper and courgette in the oil, balsamic vinegar and oregano, season well

2   Heat a cast-iron frying pan or grill to smoking hot

3   Cook the vegetables until browned and tender (about 8 minutes)

To make the sandwich

1   Toast the fennel seed khobz (see p135) on the cut sides and drizzle with olive oil

2   Layer on a couple of slices each of aubergine, red pepper and courgette and then the cheese; grill until the cheese bubbles

3   Top with a dollop of fig and date chutney (see p150)

4   Serve with a green salad

soups

Not merely sustenance, soups in Morocco are symbolic: a bridge that transports the diner from one state of consciousness to another. *Harira*, for example, breaks the fast as the sun sets during Ramadan and is served with honey-drenched sesame pastries and dates. *B'sarra* (p17), on the other hand, is a breakfast soup, always served with wake-you-up, freshly ground spices, a drizzle of oil and *khobz*. Then there are all the medicinal soups, administered for just about any kind of ailment you can think of.

Souad can knock up a soothing herbal broth to fortify pregnant women in the blink of an eye, Tariq can cure a bad case of Moroccan belly with just a small bowlful of his roasted garlic soup, and a short stroll along the Talaa K'bira will confirm that there's nothing better for a head cold than a bowl of hedgehog broth. Thyme tea, if you're a little bit squeamish, also works wonders.

There are soups to fortify the weary traveller, soups to heat your bones in the bitterly cold winters of Fez, and soups inspired by the Spanish gazpacho – one of the treats brought back after the Moors fled Andalucia – to cool you down when the sun beats down unrelentingly in the summer months. Some of these, like *harira*, are fixtures on the Clock menu, others were inspired by the stories I was told while cooking in the kitchen with Souad and Tariq.

Harira with shubkiya (sesame and honey knots), dates and khobz

Harira is eaten as evening breaks during the 30 days of Ramadan, when Muslims fast from sunrise to sunset. At the given time – decided by the minister of the moon – a cannon is fired and folks rush home to begin the evening of feasting. Every town has its own version of *harira*. Casablanca adds broad beans and lentils, Marrakech uses only lentils, and Fez uses chickpeas for everyday *harira* and one made with almonds for celebrating feasts, particularly weddings, to signify a life of abundance.

The dates of Ramadan change every year since Islam follows a lunar calendar, but the Clock serves this hearty soup all year round together with the traditional accompaniments: *shubkiya* (sweet sesame knots soaked in honey) and dates. Adding the herb paste at the end is a trick of Souad's, and keeps the aromas bright.

My version is inspired by the *phô* of Vietnam and at home I like to serve it alongside bowls of dry harissa, plenty of fresh herbs (parsley, coriander and mint) and wedges of lemon.

500 g chickpeas, cooked

1 tbsp celery tops, washed, trimmed of stalks and chopped

2 onions, diced

8 ripe tomatoes, quartered

2 tbsp cubed lamb or beef (optional)

3 tsp sweet paprika

2 heaped tsp dried, ground ginger

1 tsp saffron, gently heated and crumbled

Herb paste

1 tbsp parsley, washed, trimmed of stalks and chopped

1 tbsp coriander, washed, trimmed of stalks and chopped

salt

1   Boil the tomato quarters for 5 minutes and drain, reserving the tomato water, blend the tomato flesh then pass through a sieve to get rid of the peel

2   Put the chickpeas, onions, butter, beef or lamb, celery tops and all the spices into a large saucepan and sauté gently for 10–15 minutes

3   Add the tomatoes and the tomato water, plus enough water to cover the chickpea mix

4   Simmer gently for 1 hour

5   Pound the coriander and parsley in a pestle and mortar with a little salt to make a coarse paste

6   Finish the soup by stirring in the herb paste at the last minute

7   Serve with a wedge of lemon, bowls of fresh coriander, parsley and mint, harissa, dates, and *shubkiya*

Roasted garlic soup (serves 4) (V)

Roasting the garlic for this hot, winter soup gives it a rich, velvety texture and a sweet nutty taste. It's an unusual starter to serve before a roast leg of lamb mechouia style (p84) and harissa roast potatoes (p102). If you are freezing it, do so at stage 5 before adding the cream and Parmesan.

1   Preheat the oven to 180°C

2   Trim the bottoms of the garlic bulbs to expose just a little of the flesh, toss in 2 tbsp olive oil and bake for about 45 minutes until soft and golden. Cool, then squeeze the garlic out of the cloves and set aside

3   Melt the butter over a gentle heat and sauté the onions and thyme until golden (about 5 minutes)

4   Add the roasted garlic and the chicken stock and simmer for 20 minutes or until the garlic is very soft

5   Purée the soup until very smooth, then stir in the whipped cream, season

6   Serve with 1 tbsp Parmesan cheese dropped into the top of each bowl, a sprinkle of paprika and a wedge of lemon on the side

6 bulbs garlic, whole
2 mild white onions, sliced
2 tbsp olive oil
2 tbsp butter
1 tbsp fresh thyme
¾ litre chicken stock
½ litre cream, whipped
4 tbsp Parmesan cheese, finely grated
4 lemon wedges
1 tsp paprika
salt and pepper

Chilled broad bean and pea soup (serves 4) (V)

This soup is a springtime variation on the classic split pea *b'sarra* although it does take a bit more work. Broad beans are abundant in Morocco in the late spring and this is one of the nicest ways to eat them.

1 Blanch the broad beans and peas in a scant amount of water until just tender (about a minute and a half). Leave to cool then slip the beans from their grey outer hulls

2 Sauté the onion in olive oil until golden

3 Toss the hulled beans and peas in with the onion, stir for half a minute and add the chicken stock

4 Bring to simmer, turn off the heat and leave to cool

5 Whisk the mint into the yogurt, cover and leave to chill in the fridge for at least 30 minutes

6 Purée the soup in a hand blender or food processor until smooth, check for seasoning, sieve and chill covered for at least 30 minutes

7 Top with a dollop of minted yogurt before serving

1 kg broad beans, shelled
1 kg peas, shelled
1 mild white onion, sliced
1½ litres chicken stock
50 ml Greek yogurt
1 tbsp olive oil
1 tbsp mint, finely chopped
salt and pepper

Jajik: chilled cucumber, yogurt and mint soup (serves 4) (V)

This refreshing and energising soup is the perfect antidote to hot, Moroccan summers. Café Clock uses a Moroccan variety of cucumber, which is conveniently hollow, but the usual salad variety is just as good. Serve it with spice trader's flatbreads (p136) for a light lunch or supper.

1 Place all the ingredients except the argan oil and ground cumin in a blender and whizz until smooth

2 Cover and refrigerate overnight

3 Check for seasoning and serve cold, garnished with a couple of mint leaves, a drizzle of argan oil and a sprinkle of ground cumin

2 large cucumbers, peeled and seeded (cut into manageable lengths, split down the middle and scoop out the seeds with a teaspoon)
500 ml plain Greek yogurt
250 ml iced water
50 g walnuts, finely chopped
1 tbsp runny honey, or 2 tsp caster sugar
1 tbsp mint, finely chopped
1 tbsp argan oil
1 tsp ground cumin
salt and pepper

Cherry gazpacho (serves 4) (V)

On the whole it is true to say that the Moors probably influenced the Andaluz kitchen far more than the other way around, but this is one exception. A delightful summer party dish served in shot glasses as an elegant starter before you sit down for dinner proper. If you can't get cherries, watermelon is a good substitute and makes a lighter soup.

1   Combine the tomatoes, cherries, celery, garlic, olive oil and vinegar in a bowl, refrigerate covered overnight

2   Blend it well, until you get a smooth, thick soup

3   Check for seasoning, and chill until ready to serve

500 g ripe tomatoes, roughly chopped

500 g ripe cherries, pitted, roughly chopped

3 sticks celery, finely chopped

1 small red onion, chopped

3 garlic cloves, crushed

4 tbsp mild olive oil

3 tbsp good quality white wine vinegar

salt and pepper

fish

مربع منشور بنجمة حزلاد

وما علم الركـ

مريحة في كل الاساليب

إسلوب الرفعة وكا بوكية في

تستعمل النقط في إعط

او كوجعلة للقياس

في بداية تعلم إعط على ال

فياسا قبل الاوضاع والعر

القياس بواسطة النقطة التي

ولاجب إعط بين

و نفسها ، ودائما ما تكون ن

نقطاب ، ولا نواها على

الغطاط عند ما يسرو ل

طاطين او للتهيع للخط والت

عواكعروف و التشكيل

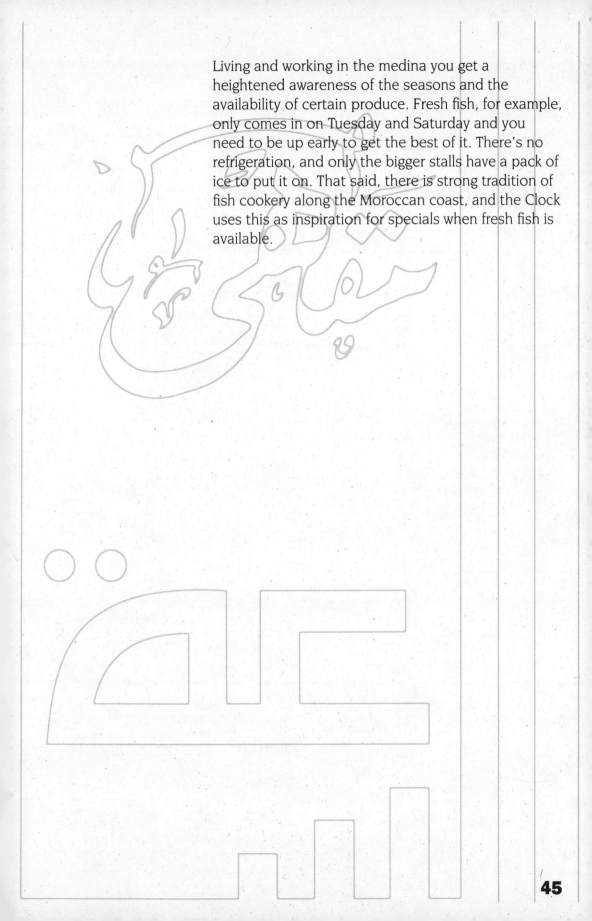

Living and working in the medina you get a heightened awareness of the seasons and the availability of certain produce. Fresh fish, for example, only comes in on Tuesday and Saturday and you need to be up early to get the best of it. There's no refrigeration, and only the bigger stalls have a pack of ice to put it on. That said, there is strong tradition of fish cookery along the Moroccan coast, and the Clock uses this as inspiration for specials when fresh fish is available.

Moules marinière Morocco style (serves 4)

You don't see mussels very often in Fez, but when you do you can bet you'll see them on the specials board later that day. Who doesn't love a bowl of moules marinière, especially with a big pile of crunchy French fries on the side?

1   Heat the oil in a large saucepan over a medium heat
2   Add the garlic, stir for 1 minute, then add the tomatoes, olives, cumin, paprika, black pepper and bay leaves. Add the vermouth or wine at this stage if using
3   Stir well, turn down to a simmer and cook for 10 minutes
4   Add the mussels, cover with a lid and cook for a further 10 minutes until the mussels have opened and are a creamy, gold colour (discard any that have not opened)
5   Sprinkle with parsley and coriander and serve immediately with wedges of lemon and French fries

2 kg mussels, well scrubbed with beards removed (if you're not particularly squeamish you don't need to remove the beard, it won't affect the taste and it keeps the mussels fresher)

1 kg tomatoes, quartered, seed removed, then diced

100 g black olives (Kalamata are good if you can't get Moroccan; do not use the canned, pitted kind – they will ruin the dish)

3 garlic cloves, crushed

1 tsp cumin

1 tsp sweet paprika

½ tsp black pepper

2 bay leaves

1 glass white vermouth such as Martini bianco or Noilly Prat (optional)

1 tbsp fresh coriander, roughly chopped

1 tbsp fresh parsley, roughly chopped

2 tbsp olive oil

1 lemon, quartered

Charmoula fish and seafood grill (serves 4)

Charmoula is the classic all-purpose seasoning of Essaouira – it can function as a marinade, dressing or sauce. Whenever you order fish there you get a bowl of it on the side for dipping. Make sure you make enough to do the same with this typically Moroccan fish grill.

1   Toss the fish and seafood together in half the charmoula
2   Heat a cast-iron grill or barbecue until piping hot
3   Place the fish, prawns and squid on first and cook for 1–2 minutes on either side
4   Add the clams and mussels and cook until they pop open
5   Serve immediately with lemon quarters and the rest of the charmoula on the side

500 g fish fillets (cod, salmon, hake, etc.), cut into finger-sized portions

8 king prawns (shells on)

4 medium sized, whole squid, cleaned

20 clams

12 mussels

400 ml green charmoula

1 lemon, quartered

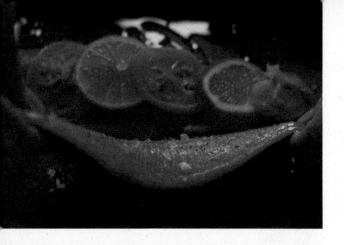

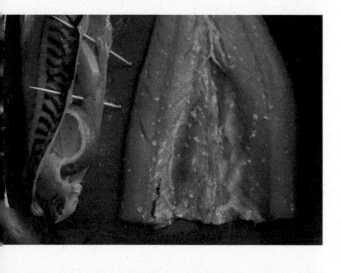

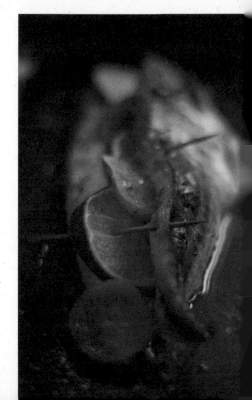

Baked mackerel with preserved lemon salsa verde (serves 4)

Oily, blue fish is plentiful in Morocco and stands up well to the strong flavours used in this dish, which is a great way to eat mackerel and something you can put together in a matter of minutes.

1 Pre-heat the oven to 200°C

2 Mix together the chopped preserved lemon, lemon juice, and coriander. Add the olive oil in a stream, stir in the olives, and chill

3 Wash the fish well and pat dry with kitchen paper

4 Slash the skin on both sides at 1-cm intervals

5 Season the cavity with salt and pepper and line with slices of preserved lemon and lime

6 Skewer the cavity together with toothpicks

7 Season the fish skin, and brush with oil

8 Bake for 30 minutes so that the skin is crisp and the flesh moist and tender

9 Serve one fillet per person with the salsa spooned over the top. Serve with rocket, orange and caper salad (see p98)

2 large mackerel, cleaned and gutted, and butterflied open

1 preserved lemon, flesh removed and discarded, half the peel finely chopped, the other half sliced

1 lime or lemon, sliced

2 tbsp fresh lemon juice

1 small bunch fresh coriander, finely chopped

1 tbsp pitted, green olives, finely chopped

3 tbsp argan or olive oil

salt and pepper

Cinnamon-rubbed fish steaks with rose petal sauce (serves 4)

You can use any meaty fish filet for this: tuna, swordfish, or better still a fillet of John Dory (St Pierre in Morocco), which is one of the best fish you will find in the Fez market. The rub for this fish is like a Moroccan version of Jamaican jerk seasoning, though we avoid the hot spices so as not to overpower the fish. It's great on the barbecue and goes brilliantly on a heap of couscous with some steamed spinach on the side.

800 g fish fillet, divided into 4 steaks
1 tbsp ground cinnamon
1 tbsp sweet paprika
1 tbsp dried thyme
2 tbsp butter
salt and pepper

Rose petal sauce
2 tbsp rose petal syrup
1 tsp cinnamon
1 tbsp olive oil
juice of 1 lemon

1   Mix together the dry spices, salt and pepper and rub them well into the fish. Set aside for at least 30 minutes

2   Melt the butter over a medium heat until foaming, then add the fish steaks. Cook for 3–4 minutes on either side, depending on the thickness of the steak and how you like your fish

3   Remove from the pan and serve with a drizzle of the rose petal sauce over the top

For the rose petal sauce

1   Whisk together all the ingredients and leave to marinate for at least 30 minutes in the fridge

Crispy fried squid with tomato and chilli chutney (serves 4)

This is one of those great mid-week suppers that you can throw together in two minutes for a gang of friends and serve with nothing more than a big, green salad and a glass of citrusy Sauvignon Blanc. At the Clock it comes in a pretty woven basket with a side of fries. Perfect.

1 Mix all the dry ingredients together

2 Wash the squid, pat dry with a kitchen towel and dredge in the flour mix until well covered

3 Fry in smoking hot oil until golden, drain on kitchen paper

4 Serve with a bowl of tomato and chilli jam on the side

500 g fresh squid rings
5 tbsp flour
3 tbsp dry harissa (p147)
1 large pinch chilli and orange infused salt (p146)
freshly ground black pepper
sunflower oil for frying

Tomato and chilli chutney
8 large ripe tomatoes, diced (or substitute 2 cans chopped Italian tomatoes)
4 cloves garlic, crushed
3 hot red chillies, sliced
2 sticks cinnamon
5 tbsp sugar
300 ml red wine vinegar

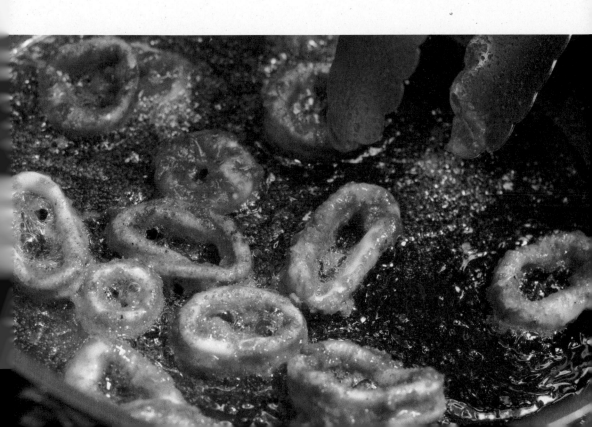

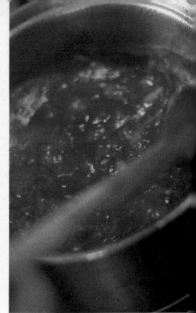

For the tomato and chilli chutney

1   Combine everything together in a pan and slowly bring to
    the boil

2   Reduce to a simmer and cook for 45 minutes, skimming
    off any residual scum

3   Pour into a sterilised jar and seal while still hot, or leave
    to cool and store in Tupperware or a jam jar where it will
    last for 2 weeks refrigerated

poultry

Chicken is a big deal in Morocco and there seem to be endless ways of preparing it. On my travels around the country I have eaten aromatic whole chicken poached in *smen* (a pungent, almost cheesy, soured butter that gives many Moroccan dishes their distinctive flavour), ginger and honey; chicken stuffed with vermicelli from a stall in the r'Cif food market; and spit-roast chicken stuffed with rice, saffron and fresh coriander in the sacred city of Moulay Idriss.

These dishes are nearly always slow-cooked as the tasty *beldi* (traditional – free-range and naturally fed) chicken tends to be tough. A trick among medina cooks is to soak chicken joints and breasts in water with lots of lemon halves over-night to tenderise it.

The Clock gets most of its chicken from Najib Djayji just around the corner from the café. He can bless, kill and pluck a chicken in the time it takes to get the rest of the vegetables for the day's dishes. Cooking in the medina is not for the squeamish, but few experiences are more vividly real or flavourful.

Chicken, preserved lemon and green olive tagine (serves 4)

Ask people what their favourite Moroccan recipe is and nine times out of ten you'll get this dish in response. Somehow it manages to be both light and sumptuous at the same time. The flavours that develop in the pot – the bitterness of olives contrasting nicely with the aromatic lemons and the sweet, buttery juices of the chicken – form an irresistible combination that deserves a place in every enthusiastic cook's repertoire.

My version of this dish was learned at the hands of Lella Latifa, whose husband has a stall selling rabbits and hedgehogs (for soup) in the medina. She makes her tagine over hot coals on a terracotta brazier, for which there is no real substitute. But you'll come a close second with a terracotta or cast iron casserole on the stovetop.

The great thing about this dish for a dinner party is that you throw it all in the pot and let the flame do all the work. In Morocco it is always eaten with the hands with lots of freshly baked *khobz*, but it is also good – though not quite the same – with plain boiled rice or couscous and a knife and fork.

1   Cover the carcass in 1 litre of water and bring to the boil with half an onion (skinned), 2 cinnamon sticks and 2 bay leaves. Simmer gently for 30 minutes until you have an aromatic stock. Strain and reserve

2   Heat the olive oil in a large terracotta casserole or a cast-iron pot

3   Fry the chicken pieces until golden

4   Add the onion, garlic, and olives and gently sauté with the chicken until they begin to soften

5   Cut the preserved lemon in half and rinse well. Remove the flesh, discard half and mash the other half. Slice the rind into thin strips.

1 whole chicken, cleaned and jointed in 12 pieces (skin-on, bone-in and a mix of breast, legs and wings) – reserve the carcass for making stock

To make the stock
1 half onion, skinned
2 cinnamon sticks
2 bay leaves

For the tagine
1 large mild onion, thinly sliced
150g green olives (preferably the moss-green cracked kind as these give most flavour, do not use canned pitted olives)
1 preserved lemon
4 cloves garlic, crushed
1 tsp ground ginger
1 tsp sweet paprika
1 tsp saffron, toasted and crushed in your palm
3 tbsp mixed fresh parsley and coriander (roughly chopped)
1 tbsp butter
2 tbsp extra virgin olive oil
salt and freshly ground pepper

6   Add the spices (ginger, paprika and saffron) and lemon
    mix to the chicken and stir well to combine

7   Cover with the chicken stock (you may not use all of it),
    turn the heat down low and simmer gently for 1 hour

8   Just before serving check for seasoning, stir in the butter
    and the herbs

9   Transfer to a tagine if you have one, garnish with the
    parsley and coriander and serve

Honey, lemon and ginger roast chicken (serves 6)

In the holy town of Moulay Idriss a version of this is served whole and stuffed with saffron rice. It makes a spectacular dinner party dish, but it's also great if you omit the stuffing and simply rub drumsticks or wings with the marinade and roast to serve cold at a picnic, or to barbecue. Cooking pot-roast style for the smaller cuts ensures the meat stays tender and juicy. Serve the juices as a gravy on the side.

1   Preheat oven to 200°C

2   Mix all the marinade ingredients together with a hand blender

3   Pierce the chicken skin by pinching the skin up away from the flesh and pushing a fork through (this way you won't damage the flesh)

4   Rub the marinade well into the chicken on all sides and beneath the skin of the breast. As the butter hardens it will give it a lovely, golden coat. Cover with foil and roast for 1 hour (if you're cooking a whole bird you could stuff it with the rice rather than serving it on the side – simply cook the rice as normal but do not steam it at the end of cooking (see p59) – it will steam inside the chicken)

5   Remove the foil and roast for another 20 minutes until the skin is golden but not burned

6   Remove from oven and leave to stand for 15 minutes before carving if serving a whole chicken

7   Serve with saffron rice

2 kg chicken (whole or in pieces)

For the marinade

150 g fresh ginger, or 2 tbsp dried ginger

juice of 1 lemon

2 tbsp runny honey

2 tbsp softened butter

1 tsp sweet paprika

1 tsp rose-petal infused salt

½ tsp fresh ground white pepper

For the saffron rice

500 g basmati rice

1 mild white onion

1 tsp saffron strands, toasted in a dry frying pan, then crushed

1 tbsp olive oil

2 tbsp parsley

1 tsp salt

To make the saffron rice

1. Sauté the onion over a medium heat until soft and golden (about 6 minutes) but not brown, then add the toasted saffron

2. Add the rice and salt and stir so it is well coated in the saffron/onion mixture

3. Cover the rice so that the water comes up to just about an inch above it

4. Bring to the boil, reduce to a simmer and cook until the water has evaporated so the surface of the rice splutters with craters

5. Turn the heat off, cover the rice with a tight-fitting lid and leave to steam for 12 minutes

R'fisa: chicken, lentil and fenugreek stew (serves 4)

Tariq was the first person to cook this dish for me and I was intrigued that I'd never come across it before. It is rarely seen in restaurants, but he explained that in Morocco r'fisa is a ceremonial dish that only comes out on special occasions.

Traditionally, it is served to expectant or new mothers as it is believed to promote both labour and lactation. The fenugreek is also believed to cleanse the body and spirit, and as such it is also served on the 15th day of Ramadan, marking the halfway point of the fast and an encouragement to keep going. It is also served on the last day of Ramadan, the first day of Eid, and always for the prophet Mohammed's birthday.

In Morocco it is eaten with *trid* – a delicate, flaky flatbread – but it is also good with plain basmati rice.

1   Combine the marinade ingredients and rub well into the chicken, place in a zip-lock bag and leave to marinate overnight

To make the *r'fisa* stew

1   Remove the chicken from the marinade, shake off the excess and sauté the chicken in olive oil in a large, heavy-bottomed pan, until golden. Remove the chicken pieces and set aside

2   Sauté the onions and garlic in the same pan with the chicken juices, adding a splash more oil if needed. Fry until golden

3   Add the tomatoes, ground ginger, ras al hanout, turmeric, saffron, salt and pepper to taste, and cook for 2–3 minutes until well combined

4   Add the fenugreek and lentils, return the chicken to the pan, just cover with water and bring to the boil

5   Turn the heat down low, add the fresh herbs and simmer for an hour (if it starts to look too dry add a little more water)

6   When the lentils and fenugreek are tender, check for seasoning and transfer to a serving dish. Sprinkle with more fresh herbs and serve with *trid* (p138) and lemon quarters

1.5 kg beldi or organic chicken, jointed

For the marinade
4 tbsp Dijon mustard
4 tbsp ground ginger
1 tbsp chilli powder
2 tbsp plain flour
juice of 5 lemons
2 tsp salt

For the r'fisa stew
3 large, red onions, halved and thinly sliced
2 large tomatoes, halved and thinly sliced
12 cloves garlic, skin on
large bunch of parsley and coriander, roughly chopped
100 g fenugreek simmered in hot water for 3 minutes to remove the bitterness, drain
100 g green lentils
2 tsp ras al hanout
1 tbsp ground ginger
1 tsp turmeric
pinch saffron
3 tbsp olive oil
3 tbsp vegetable oil
1 litre water
salt and pepper

القـ

PAPRIKA
DOUX

الكا

كوزة حبشية
للتبخير

خل

POIVRE
NOIR

GENGOMBRE

4
EPICES

35483
5094
7438
2344

POIVRE
BLANC

الخرقوم

Duck in spiced pomegranate molasses with cherries (serves 2)

This is one of those easy, no-fuss dinner party dishes that your guests will think you've been slaving over for hours. This isn't something that is served at the Clock, but it was inspired by a version of duck tagine that Tariq told me about.

2 large duck breasts
50 g dried sour cherries, halved
6 cardamom pods, crushed
2 star anise
1 cinnamon stick
juice of 2 large pomegranates

1   Combine the pomegranate juice, spices and sour cherries in a pan and bring to a boil; turn to a simmer until reduced by half, leave to cool (this can be done the night before)

2   Score the skin of the duck breast (taking care not to damage the meat) and then place in a zip-lock bag with the marinade for at least 2 hours

3   Preheat the oven to 180°

4   Shake the excess marinade off the duck, reserving the rest, then dry fry the duck skin-side down over a medium heat until the skin is golden and much of the fat has rendered (remove the fat but conserve it for roasting potatoes another time). Turn over and fry for another 2 minutes to seal the flesh, then place in a baking tray flesh-side down. Pour over the reserved marinade and place in the oven for 5 minutes (for medium rare), or a bit longer if you prefer it more well done

5   Serve drizzled with the pomegranate juices, with a watercress salad on the side

Roast, spiced quail with pistachio and mint chutney (serves 4)

This dish also works well with lamb or chicken and is great on the barbecue. Serve it with olive oil mashed potatoes and some steamed green beans.

1   Combine all of the spice, orange and lemon zest and salt together with the oil and rub well into the poultry

2   Place in a zip-lock bag and leave to marinade in the fridge for 2 hours, or preferably overnight

3   Place the spatchcocked quail or poussins (alternatively you could leave them whole and roast them at 200° for 20–30 minutes) under a medium-hot grill for 5–8 minutes either side, or until the outside is crisp and golden and the inside tender and juicy

To make the chutney

1   Combine all the ingredients

2   Refrigerate in an airtight container for at least an hour before serving. The chutney will keep in this way in the fridge for up to a week.

8 quail or 4 poussin, spatchcocked

2 tbsp orange zest

1 tbsp lemon zest

2 dried chillies, crumbled

1 tsp ground cinnamon

1 tsp ground cardamom

1 tsp ground allspice

½ tsp turmeric

½ tsp orange and chilli infused salt

4 tbsp olive oil

For the chutney

150 g shelled pistachios, chopped

2 tbsp rosewater

2 tbsp fresh mint, well chopped

2 cloves garlic, crushed

1 tbsp runny honey

juice of 1 lemon

drizzle olive oil

salt, to taste

63

Couscous boohaloo (serves 4)

This is the dish that was served the day the Clock opened, at their *abbassiya*, the traditional dinner held for friends and neighbours when you open a new business in Morocco.

The Clock uses couscous from the tiny mud village of Douar El Khoukhate, where it is rolled by hand from wheat grown and harvested by ENNAHDA, an all women cooperative aided by the Peace Corps. They grow the wheat, harvest and grind it themselves, and then mix it with water from the spring that gives the couscous its name, karma (meaning fig tree in Darija), which results in a rich, nutty couscous unlike anything you've had before. Assuming hand-rolled couscous is not to hand, use wholewheat for best results.

250 g wholewheat couscous
4 large chicken legs and thighs
1 large onion, diced
4 cloves garlic, crushed
3 tsp ground ginger
1 tsp ground black pepper
1 tsp salt
1 tsp herb paste (see p38)
2 tbsp olive oil
2 tbsp vegetable oil
1 tbsp almonds, toasted
1 tbsp dried apricots, poached in plain water until soft and tender

For the caramelised onion and raisin jam

2 onions, finely sliced
1 tbsp raisins
1 tbsp vegetable oil
1 tsp saffron, heated and crumbled
½ tsp ground black pepper
1 tsp ground ginger
1 tsp brown sugar
½ tsp ground cinnamon
50 ml water

1   Cover the couscous in cold water and stir around with your hands, adding just enough liquid to make a crumb but not to soak it

2   Set aside and mix with the hands from time to time (if it seems like it's drying out add more liquid). This tenderises the couscous and lets the grain open up, releasing the delicate flavours

3   Mix together the onions, garlic, ginger, pepper, salt, herb paste, olive and vegetable oil and rub well into the chicken

4   Place the chicken in large, heavy-bottomed pan, cover and cook over a medium heat for an hour, stirring once in a while

5   Check the couscous, which should now feel soft, springy and cool to the touch. Add a dash of mild olive oil and place in a steamer (if you don't have a steamer, use a stainless steel sieve over a pan of water)

6   Steam uncovered for 30 minutes, take off the heat, sprinkle with cold water and set aside

7   Check the chicken for seasoning, pile the couscous into a tagine or large shallow dish and arrange the chicken on top spooned over with onion and raisin jam

8   Sprinkle with toasted almonds; poached, dried apricots and a small dish of the chicken juices on the side

9   Serve with an orange and black olive salad (see p95)

To make caramelised onion and raisin jam

1   Add the onions, raisins and spices to a saucepan

2   Cover with half an inch of water, place on a low heat and cook for an hour

3   Season with the sugar and cinnamon, and cook for a further 5 minutes before serving

meat

If chicken is your day-to-day protein in Morocco, meat is very much for special occasions, eaten in small quantities and often sweetened with dried fruits and spices.

The most revered and expensive meat of all is in fact camel – particularly the hump, which is considered a delicacy. Slowly, it is starting to appear on international menus as interest in exotic meat grows, so who knows, you may be lucky enough to get your hands on some to make your own camel hump pasty (p87) one of these days.

Elsewhere, Moroccan meat dishes are richly flavoured with herbs and spices, and, with the exception of kebabs, nearly always slow-cooked – be it *tangia* (p76) or *mechouia* (p84) – so the meat is butter tender and falling from the bone, ready to be dipped in shallow dishes of freshly ground salt, cumin and harissa. Once eaten this way, your Sunday roast will never seem quite the same again.

Fassi kebabs (serves 4)

The Clock serves these kebabs on the rooftop using a traditional Moroccan *mejmer* (a large, terracotta brazier) filled with white-hot coals. Plates of marinated meat, kefta, chicken and vegetables are served separately so that guests can make and grill their own at the table, along with a selection of salads. The marinade mix used here is typical of Fez and surrounding regions.

Mixed meat kebabs

1 Combine the meat and spices and marinate for a minimum of 1 hour; thread on to metal skewers

2 Light barbecue, if using, and allow to burn down until you get a white-hot glow on the coals (if you are using a hot grill cover the kebabs in foil for the first 3–5 minutes, and cook for another 3–5 minutes uncovered to brown)

Lamb kefta

1 Combine the meat and spices and marinate for a minimum of 1 hour

2 Squeeze small handfuls of kefta around the wooden skewers to form sausages of meat

3 Grill over charcoal (or under a hot grill) for 7–10 minutes, turning regularly to ensure they are evenly cooked

Fish and vegetable kebabs

1 Marinate the fish and vegetables in the charmoula for a minimum of 1 hour, thread on to metal skewers

2 Light barbecue, if using, and allow to burn down until you get a white-hot glow on the coals (if you are using a hot grill cover the kebabs in foil for the first 3–5 minutes, and cook for another 3–5 minutes uncovered to brown)

Kebab salsa

1 Mix the ingredients together and serve immediately (do not allow it to sit for too long or the tomatoes will go mushy)

Mixed meat kebabs

250 g each chicken, lamb, beef, cut into ½ inch cubes

4 tbsp parsley, chopped

4 tbsp onions, finely chopped

1 tbsp paprika

½ tsp cumin, ground

4 tbsp olive oil

1 tsp sea salt

1 tsp black pepper

Lamb kefta

500 g minced lamb

1 medium onion, grated

2 tbsp parsley, finely chopped

1 tbsp mint, finely chopped

1 tbsp paprika

1 tsp dried rose petals, crumbled

1 tsp black pepper

1 tsp sea salt

1 tsp olive oil

½ tsp cumin

Fish and vegetable kebabs

250 g meaty fish like monkfish, tuna or swordfish

Selection of vegetables (peppers, courgettes, aubergines, garlic, onions, cherry tomatoes) cut into ½ inch dice

5 tbsp red charmoula (see p147)

Kebab salsa

3 large ripe tomatoes, finely diced

2 hot chillies, finely chopped (optional)

3 tbsp onions, finely chopped

2 tbsp parsley, finely chopped

½ tsp sea salt

½ tsp black pepper

juice of half a lemon

2 tbsp olive oil

Beef kefta with tomato and yogurt sauce (serves 4)

Kefta are found all over Morocco and the Middle East and rank among spaghetti Bolognese, chicken curry and boeuf bourguignon as a classic dish. They are supremely versatile, special enough for a dinner party, easy enough for a mid-week supper, and freeze easily. They generally appear at the Clock chalked up as a special, especially during the damp winter months when we are all craving comfort food. Serve with rice, on pasta, or with hot pitta bread as a burger patty; in stuffed vegetables or as pie filling. The rose petals – if you can find them – give it an extra special helping of love.

1   Sauté the onions and garlic in olive oil until soft and translucent, add the beef and fry until browned

2   Add the rest of the dry ingredients and cook gently until the mix smells fragrant, remove from the heat and allow to cool slightly

3   Mix in the eggs and knead well with your hands, shape into balls, cover and chill for 20 minutes or so before cooking

4   Cook the kefta in a little oil for 3–4 minutes on either side or until well browned (insert a toothpick to check for doneness – if it emerges clean it's cooked through)

5   Serve on top of the tomato sauce, with the yogurt dressing drizzled over the top

For the tomato sauce

1   Gently fry the tomatoes, cinnamon, salt and sugar in olive oil for 10–15 minutes until thick

2   Stir in the ras al hanout 2–3 minutes before the end of cooking

For the yoghurt sauce

1   Combine all of the ingredients and chill for 30 minutes before serving to allow the flavours to develop

500 g minced beef

4 garlic cloves, crushed

1 sweet, white onion, finely diced

1 tbsp fresh coriander, finely chopped

1 tbsp fresh flat-leaf parsley, finely chopped

2 tbsp dried rose petals, finely crumbled (if you can't get rose petals use 2 tsp rose essence, or 2 tbsp rosewater)

2 tbsp sweet paprika

1 tbsp ground coriander

2 tsp cinnamon

zest of 1 lemon

zest of 1 orange

½ tsp sea salt

freshly ground black pepper

2 eggs, beaten

2 tbsp olive oil for frying

Tomato sauce

2 cans chopped tomatoes

1 tbsp olive oil

1 tsp cinnamon

1 tsp ras al hanout

½ tsp salt

½ tsp sugar

Yoghurt sauce

200 ml thick plain yogurt

2 garlic cloves, crushed

1 tbsp tahini

1 tbsp lemon juice

Fassi-style tangia (serves 4)

This is the ultimate comfort food and needs to be ordered 24 hours in advance if you want to eat it at the Clock. Traditionally, *tangia* (named for the terracotta urn in which it is cooked) is one of the few dishes cooked by the men of the medina and they guard their recipes fiercely. Until that is, Gail Leonard, the creator of Fez Food and collaborator on the Clock Kitchen Cooking School, started making enquiries about it.

As she was shuttled from trader to trader, taken to the best butcher for meat (in Marrakech it's lamb, in Fez always beef and with onions) and newspaper-wrapped packets of secret spices were slipped between her palms, their secrets came tumbling out. Ever since, whenever Gail trundles down the main artery of the medina, Talaa K'bira, where she lives, with a pram and a *tangia* where a baby should be, she's been known simply as *ukhti* – a term of endearment meaning 'dear sister' – *tangia*. In the blink of an eye she went from *gouria* (foreign woman) in the souk, to a bona fide part of the community.

As with most traditional recipes, there are myriad ways of cooking it: the meat is always bought from the butcher first thing in the morning, along with freshly ground spices. Together with sliced red onions and a scrap of preserved lemon the whole lot is packed into the *tangia*, sealed with a foil top and taken to one of the local hammams – the *ferran* (bread oven) is too hot – then left to sit in the embers for 4 or 5 hours, slowly cooking away until the meat is fragrant, meltingly tender and spiked with the smokiness of the wood fire.

As most people don't have a hammam on their doorstep, I've adapted Gail's recipe for a normal oven.

2 kg beef on the bone, cut into 1–2 inch chunks (osso bucco is great for this, but use stewing steak if you don't like bones)

2 onions, roughly chopped

1 preserved lemon, quartered then rinsed (include both flesh and skin)

6 cloves of garlic, whole

2 tbsp fresh ginger, grated

2 tbsp ground cumin

2 tsp ground black pepper

1 tbsp ras el hanout

1 tsp saffron threads

5 bay leaves

1 small bunch each fresh coriander and parsley (including stalks)

250 ml water (or white wine if you prefer – don't use red, it overpowers the flavours)

50 ml olive oil

1 Preheat oven to 50°C

2 Mix all of the ingredients together with your hands, rubbing the spices well into the meat

3 Pack into a large terracotta or cast-iron casserole dish with a lid and leave to cook gently for up to 6 hours, stirring occasionally to prevent from sticking (add a splash more water from time to time if it starts to look dry)

4 Serve straight from the pot with plenty of bread for mopping up the juices, or a side of mashed potatoes

Note

If your oven only goes down to 95°C, reduce cooking time to 4–5 hours

Variation

Curiously enough, especially given Fez's distance from the sea, another speciality of the area is fish *tangia*. Simply substitute with meaty fish fillets (tuna, swordfish, monkfish are all good) and mix with the juice of 2 lemons, turmeric, paprika, cumin and freshly crushed garlic. Cook for only 2 hours otherwise the fish will collapse completely.

Harissa beef (serves 4)

This is a great way of making a little beef go a long way. The harissa marinade gives an otherwise fairly boring cut of meat a beautiful, sweet and spicy crust that acts to seal in the juices. A herb-based honey like thyme or rosemary is ideal for this savoury dish, but any runny honey will do. I like to serve it 'Thai style' but using Moroccan flavours. Cook the beef rare, slice thinly and then toss with plenty of bitter leaves like frisée, rocket and watercress, fresh mint and coriander, slivers of red onion and red chillies, and some sun-dried tomatoes. Drizzle over some red charmoula (p147) and finish with a squeeze of lemon.

300 g fillet of beef
2 tsp dry harissa
2 tbsp sunflower oil
1 tbsp runny honey
1 tsp sea salt
1 tsp black pepper (freshly ground, not powdered)

1   Preheat oven to 200°C

2   Mix together the harissa, oil, honey, salt and pepper to create an emulsion

3   Pat the beef dry with a kitchen towel, then rub the spice mixture well into the meat with your hands

4   Sear the beef in a smoking hot pan, turning now and then so that it develops a dark, caramelised crust all over

5   Place on the middle shelf of the oven and finish off by roasting for 5 minutes (medium rare), 7–8 minutes (well done)

6   Remove and leave to rest for 5 minutes before slicing thinly if serving hot. If serving cold, leave to cool and slice as needed to keep the meat moist

Beef terrine with prunes and pistachios (serves 4)

This takes a little bit of work, and as such doesn't appear on the Clock menu terribly often. It's inspired by the liver sausages that you see being chopped up into hot sandwiches in the evening at the top of Talaa K'bira and by the flavours more traditionally used in a beef and prune tagine. It's a great dish to have in the fridge for a quick 'Ploughman's' lunch or supper, with *khobz*, chutney and salad.

- 1 kg beef mince
- 250 g free-range chicken livers, roughly chopped
- 1 onion, finely chopped
- 5 or 6 sprigs thyme
- 6 fresh sage leaves, finely chopped
- ½ tsp ground nutmeg
- 2 tsp five-spice mix
- 4 tbsp brandy or Calvados (optional)
- 200 ml red wine or chicken stock
- 50 g shelled pistachio nuts
- 6 prunes, pitted and sliced
- 1 tbsp olive oil
- 1 tbsp butter (for greasing the pan)

1 Combine the mince, livers, herbs and spices in a bowl, season and knead in the brandy. Cover and rest in the fridge overnight

2 Preheat oven to 200°C and prepare a roasting tray two-thirds full with water to make a bain-marie

3 Fry the onion gently in the olive oil until soft and translucent. Add the wine or stock and reduce over a low heat for a few minutes until thick. Leave to cool, then add the chilled meat mix, the pistachio nuts and prunes, stir well

4 Grease a 20 cm terrine mould or loaf tin with butter, line with greaseproof paper, then pack in the terrine mix, pushing it right into the corners; lightly brush with olive oil

5 Carefully place the terrine in the middle of the bain-marie and bake for 45 minutes to 1 hour (if a skewer inserted into the middle emerges clean, it's cooked)

6 Cool in the tin before carefully turning out. Store whole and cut into slices as needed

Lamb, saffron and ginger tagine with pears (serves 4)

In Morocco, mutton tagine is generally made with quince, which are in season from October to December. You can't eat them raw, but they taste quite wonderful once they've been boiled and added to this decadent-looking dish. This version of the Moroccan classic is a little bit milder in flavour and made using ingredients that are easier to find. Tender spring lamb goes particularly well with pears since they don't overpower the delicate taste of the meat. They do, however, pick up the scent of the spices nicely, and add a gentle sweetness to the stew.

400 g lamb, cut into chunks

1 sweet white onion, finely chopped

8 small, whole peeled pears

2 cinnamon sticks

2 tsp dried ginger

1 tsp saffron strands, heated then crumbled between the palm

100 g toasted almonds, peeled

50 g natural yogurt (ideally Greek for thickness)

handful fresh coriander leaves

1 tbsp olive oil

1 tsp salt

1   Steam the pears in a little water with two cinnamon sticks until tender; leaving in the liquid, set aside to cool

2   Sauté the lamb and onions in olive oil until browned

3   Add the ginger, saffron, salt and just cover with water

4   Turn the heat down as low as it will go and cook gently for about 2 hours

5   Toast the almonds and set aside

6   At the end of cooking the tagine should be a golden colour. Reheat the pears, remove from the liquid and stud with almonds

7   Transfer the meat to a large tagine, or to 4 individual tagines, arranging the pears around it. Spoon the juices over the top

8   Scatter with a handful of torn coriander, and a dollop of yogurt

9   Serve immediately with a selection of Moroccan breads and a crisp, green salad

Roast lamb mechouia style (serves 4)

The smell alone of this dish is enough to get you salivating, and by the time it emerges from a slow oven it's maddening. No wonder it's traditionally torn apart with the fingers and eaten with no embellishment. Although this isn't yet available at the Clock, it's included as one of Morocco's finest dishes. Shoulder works better than leg as it is fattier so you get tender flesh running with juices and a delicious, crispy skin. Serve it with dishes of the juice, and freshly ground cumin, sea salt and dry harissa for dipping.

2 kg lamb shoulder
180 g butter
10 garlic cloves, crushed
1 tbsp cumin seeds, crushed
1 tbsp coriander seeds, ground
1 tsp turmeric
1 tsp ginger, ground
1 g saffron
salt and pepper

1 Combine the butter and spices together and chill overnight

2 Preheat oven to 220°C

3 Wash and dry the lamb, slash crosswise to score the skin (avoid cutting the flesh), then rub the spiced butter into the lamb and roast on the middle shelf for 30 minutes until the skin begins to turn a golden brown

4 Turn the oven down to 140°C, cover the lamb in foil and continue roasting for another 3 hours

5 Transfer to a board with the foil still on and leave to rest for 10 minutes before carving, serving the pan juices on the side (if they are a little on the scant side add a splash of water or white wine and heat through on the stove before serving)

Rabbit and apricot b'stilla (serves 4)

If you eat at any of the palace restaurants in Fez or Marrakech, *b'stilla* – specifically pigeon *b'stilla* – is nearly always part of the menu. It's a celebratory dish comprising pigeon with almonds, wrapped up in a crisp, pastry crust and decorated with icing sugar and cinnamon. Providing you go easy on these last two, they are a surprisingly tasty addition to the finished dish.

The Clock makes different *b'stilla* pretty much depending on the whim of whoever is making it. It works well with just about everything, though my personal favourites are seafood (served with lots of hot chilli sauce) and this more unusual one of rabbit and apricots. The list of ingredients looks long, but in fact it's very simple to make. Individual-sized pies go down a storm at drinks parties.

1   Poach the rabbit for 20 minutes in simmering water with the bay leaves and black peppercorns, drain and cool, then shred the meat off the bones with your fingers

2   Sauté the onions, cinnamon sticks, coriander, parsley, apricots, saffron, ginger, turmeric, salt, pepper and sugar until soft and golden. Stir in the almonds and remove from the heat

3   Add the rabbit meat, saffron and the orange blossom water and continue to cook for another 5 minutes before stirring in the eggs (they will cook in the heat of the mix), remove from the heat and leave to cool, discarding the cinnamon sticks

1 whole rabbit, cut into sections

3 bay leaves

5 black peppercorns

3 tbsp olive oil

2 white onions, finely chopped

2 cinnamon sticks

2 tbsp fresh coriander, roughly chopped

2 tbsp fresh parsley, roughly chopped

50 g dried apricots, thinly sliced

1 tsp saffron threads, toasted and crumbled

1 tsp ground ginger

½ tsp turmeric

1 tbsp sugar

100 g flaked almonds, roughly chopped

4 eggs, lightly beaten

1 tbsp orange blossom water

6 large warka, or filo sheets

50 g unsalted butter, melted

salt and pepper

To assemble the b'stilla

1   Preheat oven to 190°C with rack in the middle of the oven

2   Layer the warka sheets one on top of the other with a sheet of clingfilm between each; cover the lot with a dampened tea towel (this will keep them from drying out while you work with them)

3   Take one sheet of warka, brush with melted butter and transfer to a baking tray lined with baking paper and repeat with the next two sheets of warka, arranging them slightly skewed so that the edges form a star shape

4   Spread the rabbit mix around the centre of the warka and out to about an inch away from the edge and draw the edges of the pastry up around it

5   Butter the last remaining sheets of warka as for the base of the pie, and arrange on top of the meat in the same star shape tucking the edges underneath the pie. Gently press down to flatten, brush the surface with melted butter, flip and brush the other side with butter, then flip back (smooth side up).

6   Bake for 30 minutes or until golden brown, turning over halfway through; remove and lightly dust with icing sugar and ground cinnamon laid out in a star shape. Omit this step if you don't like the sweetness, the pie is just as good without it

Camel hump pasty (makes 4)

For many, camel hump is the most delicious part of the animal. My point of conversion came when Souad suggested a Moroccan-style pasty as the best way to eat it. It's unlikely you'll come across much camel hump in your local butcher, but it may well become the snack of the future in the medina of Fez.

1   Mix the flours together and make a well. Pour in the yeast, salt and a little warm water. Allow the yeast to melt and then knead to form a dough. Roll into 8 small balls and leave to rise

2   Meanwhile, heat the olive oil and fry the onions, parsley, garlic, hump fat and, if using, the dried camel meat, until soft. Add the spices and chopped olives. Take off the heat and add the oregano.

3   Take two of the dough balls and flatten each to the size of a side plate, around 1.5 cm thick. On one, place some of the stuffing mixture and cover with the other, rolling up the sides and pinching together to make a pasty. Rub some of the juice from the stuffing mix on the top of the pasty then brush with whisked egg and a drizzle of olive oil.

4   Bake for 20–25 minutes until golden brown.

For the dough
200 g white flour
200 g wholemeal flour
2 tbsp fresh yeast
1 tsp salt

For the stuffing
2 finely chopped onions
one large bunch chopped flat-leaf parsley
150 g camel hump fat cut into small cubes – if can't get the hump (!) you could use beef fat
50 g dried camel meat khlee, shredded (optional)
one whole head of garlic, chopped
1 tsp chilli powder
1 tsp paprika
½ tsp cumin
½ tsp ras el hanout
4 tbsp sliced green olives
2 tbsp dried oregano

For the glaze
2–3 whole eggs, whisked
good-quality olive oil

salads and sides

Salads are a quintessential part of the meal in Morocco though they aren't necessarily what we might think of as salad in the West. More accurately they come as a selection of small, tapas-style vegetable dishes, which will nearly always include some spiced aubergine, a dish of aromatic stewed red and green peppers, perhaps some tender, steamed beetroot doused with yogurt and cumin, a sweet tomato confit and courgettes sautéed in *za'atar* (see p146). Sweet, sour, salty, spicy, fried and steamed then, Moroccan salads cover just about every fix your tastebuds could desire.

Some of these dishes are traditional, others are reworked for a lighter result. Whichever your preference, you'll find they require no more effort than tossing a few ingredients together, and many work equally well as a side or a main course.

Lobia (white beans in tomato sauce) (serves 4)

Lobia is a general term used for white beans and comes in various guises. Basically there are as many recipes for it as there are cooks who make it. This is Souad's version, a sort of Moroccan baked beans, which I like to serve in earthenware bowls with lots of warm *khobz* for mopping up the juices.

300 g white beans such as cannelini

2 tomatoes, chopped

1 white onion, finely diced

3 cloves garlic, crushed

2 tbsp olive oil

1 tsp black pepper, ground

1 tsp ginger, ground

1 tsp salt

1 tsp paprika

½ tsp cayenne pepper

½ litre chicken stock

1 tbsp fresh coriander, roughly chopped

1 tbsp fresh parsley, roughly chopped

1   Soak the beans overnight, then cook until tender (about 2 hours) or substitute canned beans

2   Fry the onions, garlic, tomatoes, black pepper, ginger, salt, paprika and cayenne pepper together in a saucepan until they begin to caramelise (about 10 minutes)

3   Add the beans, stir for a minute and cover over with the chicken stock (you do not need to use all of it)

4   Simmer gently until the sauce is thick and the beans soft and buttery in texture (about 20 minutes)

5   Add the coriander and parsley and cook for a further 2 minutes

6   Garnish with a sprig of parsley or coriander and serve with plenty of *khobz* and lemon wedges

Variation

If you're serving this dish as a tapa, mash it down with a fork when it's cold to make a coarse paté that goes well on crackers or crisp flatbread.

Bean and spinach stew (serves 4)

I first came across this dish at a roadside stall in the Atlas Mountains and it was made with chard, not spinach. I thought it was so tasty and comforting that I find myself craving it on many a cold winter's day in Fez. The Clock usually has something similar on the go.

1 Sauté the onion, garlic and red pepper in oil until soft and translucent

2 Add the tomatoes, tomato purée, oregano, salt and pepper and cook over a medium heat for a further 10 minutes, or until starting to caramelise

3 Add the stock and bring to the boil

4 Add the beans, reduce to a simmer and cook until the sauce has reduced to a thick, stewy consistency

5 Add the spinach and cook through for 3–4 minutes

6 Serve with plenty of *khobz* (the goat's cheese, oregano and preserved lemon is a good match, see p135)

250 g cooked white beans
1 onion, finely chopped
1 red pepper, roughly chopped
3 cloves garlic, crushed
450 g tomatoes chopped (or use 1 can)
1 tbsp tomato purée
3 tbsp olive oil
½ tsp dried oregano
large bunch spinach, washed, de-stemmed and sliced into thin strips
750 ml vegetable stock
salt and freshly ground black pepper

Shlada del barba (beetroot salad) (serves 4) (V)

Beetroot is a wonder food, packed with antioxidants, and in Morocco is believed to cleanse the spirit and ward off the mischief of the jinn. It comes in various guises and the Clock does a particularly good one for all the contrasting tastes and textures. Traditionally this dish would be sprinkled with icing sugar and cinnamon, but the Clock prefers to add cooling yogurt instead. If you don't like beetroot, try this dish with carrots, or a mix of any root vegetables.

1 Preheat the oven to 180°C

2 Mix the cumin seeds and the fennel seeds together, and set aside 1 tsp to use later

3 Toss the beetroot with the rest of the seeds and the oil, place in an oven tray and roast for 45 minutes or until tender, leave to cool

4 Transfer to a serving dish, toss with the orange blossom water and lemon juice, and top with a dollop of yogurt sprinkled with the remaining seeds

3 whole beetroot, peeled and cut into wedges
2 tsp cumin seeds, toasted and crushed in a pestle and mortar
2 tsp fennel seeds, toasted and crushed in a pestle and mortar
3 tbsp olive oil
2 tbsp orange blossom water
juice of half a lemon
salt and pepper
25 ml Greek yogurt

Zaalouk (aubergine salad) (serves 4) (V)

If hummus is the quintessential dipping sauce of
the Middle East, aubergine salads and purees are
the showcase of Morocco. This dish is smoky, silky
and creamy and perfect for vegetable crudités or
flatbreads. It's also a really good side dish to serve
with grilled lamb chops, and works just as well cold as
it does warm.

2 aubergines, sliced into half
approx ¼ cm thick

5 tbsp olive oil

3 deseeded tomatoes, cut into
eighths

4 cloves garlic, crushed

2 tbsp parsley leaves, roughly
chopped

2 tsp paprika

1 tsp cumin

½ tsp black pepper

½ tsp chilli powder (optional)

juice of 1 lemon

salt and pepper

1   Heat the olive oil in a frying pan until smoking hot (this
    prevents the aubergines from soaking up too much oil
    when you fry them)

2   Add the aubergines to the oil in small batches and fry
    until golden brown, transfer to a large salad bowl

3   Add the parsley to the still hot oil so that it crisps slightly,
    followed by the garlic and tomatoes. Stir for a minute
    then add the aubergines, cumin, paprika and lemon juice

4   Continue to cook over a high heat for a minute or two,
    breaking up the aubergines as you do so

5   Transfer to a serving platter and garnish with parsley

Ginger, pistachio and carrot salad (serves 4) (V)

This is my 'slaw'-inspired variation on the candied carrot salad so popular in Morocco. This instantly makes you feel light, healthy and raring to go.

1 Whisk together the ras al hanout, oil, lemon juice and fresh ginger to make a dressing
2 Toss with the carrots, sprinkle with pistachio nuts and coriander and serve immediately

200 g grated carrots
50 g shelled pistachios, lightly toasted
2 tsp Ras al Hanout
2 tbsp argan or nut oil
1 lemon, juiced
2 cm fresh ginger, grated
1 tbsp roughly chopped coriander

Fassi 'Waldorf' with honey yogurt dressing (serves 4) (V)

This salad goes brilliantly with fish and chicken dishes, and it's special enough to serve as a light lunch for friends.

1 Split the fennel bulbs in half, slice thinly, toss in the lemon juice and argan/walnut oil and set aside
2 Melt the butter until it foams, add 1 tbsp honey and stir for 30 seconds. Add the walnuts and cook until they are thoroughly coated in the honey/butter mix
3 Turn on to a plate and leave to cool (the honey paste will harden on them)
4 Toss the fennel with the grapes and walnuts
5 Whisk together the yogurt and 1 tbsp honey and drizzle over the top of the salad

2 fresh fennel bulbs, well cleaned with the tough outer leaves removed
juice of half a lemon
1 tbsp argan or walnut oil
50 g walnuts
2 tbsp honey
2 tbsp butter
2 tbsp thick yogurt
50 g green grapes, halved with seeds removed

Olive and orange salad (serves 4) (V)

The Clock serves this refreshing salad with barbecued meat dishes and couscous. The bright flavours really wake up your taste buds.

1 Toss everything together in a bowl
2 Serve immediately

2 oranges, peeled and segmented
50 g meaty, black olives, stones removed
1 tbsp argan oil
1 tsp sweet paprika
½ tsp sea salt

Pomegranate, beetroot and red onion salad (serves 4) (V)

This salad was inspired one balmy evening in October when Mike and I had snuck off to the Batha Hotel for a drink in their courtyard. As we sipped our gin and tonics I saw the most amazing pomegranate tree I have ever seen, its branches dripping with crimson fruit. It must have been a Persian species, which has bitter seeds, because the fruit in the markets is more of a salmon colour, though the seeds are like rubies and dazzlingly sweet. Beetroot was also in season, so the next day Tariq and I set about creating a salad that would bring the two together and make a good seasonal special for the Clock. It's a wonderful starter, but it also goes really well as a side to a thick, juicy chunk of harrissa beef (p80).

1kg small, fresh beetroot, peeled and cut into wedges

1 red onion, peeled and cut into thin wedges

12 garlic cloves, with the skin on

3 tbsp olive oil

3 tbsp balsamic vinegar

1 pomegranate (top and tail it with a sharp knife, score the tough skin and split in half, holding the cut side down over a bowl and gently hit the skin with a wooden spoon – the seeds will drop clean away)

100g feta cheese, cut into cubes

walnuts, toasted

sea salt

1   Preheat the oven to 200°C

2   Line a baking tray with foil, leaving enough excess to form a packet

3   Scatter the beetroot and garlic on top, toss with the oil, salt and vinegar, then wrap up in the foil

4   Bake for 30 minutes, remove the top layer of foil and brown off for a further 10 minutes, leave to cool

5   Toss together with the onion and pomegranate seeds

6   Scatter on the cheese and garnish with walnuts

Sumac salad (serves 4) (V)

Sumac is a Middle Eastern ingredient that comes from the dried ground berries of a shrub called *Rhus coriaria*. As a spice it is a pretty purplish-red colour with a tart, faintly lemony tang.

1   Preheat the oven to 200°C

2   Wash and dry the peppers then place them in the oven for 10–15 minutes or until the skin blackens. Remove, place in a plastic bag and leave to cool

3   When cool rub off the skins from the peppers and cut into thin strips

4   Halve the red onion and slice thinly

5   Heat 1 tbsp olive oil and sauté the onion until softened, add the red wine vinegar and the sugar and continue to cook until caramelised

6   Toss the chickpeas, peppers, red onion and chillies together in a bowl

7   Add the 1 tbsp olive oil and the lemon juice and toss again

8   Add the cheese, the parsley and the coriander and gently stir through the chickpea mix, taking care not to break up the cheese

9   Sprinkle with sumac and serve

500 g cooked, drained chickpeas
2 red peppers
1 red onions, sliced
1–2 red chillies, sliced
1 tbsp red wine vinegar
2 tbsp olive oil
200 g hard goat's cheese, or feta, cubed
2 tbsp fresh parsley
2 tbsp fresh coriander
juice of 1 lemon
1 tbsp sumac

Rocket, orange and caper salad (serves 4) (V)

This salad really couldn't be simpler and its peppery, citrusy flavours go exceptionally well with fish dishes like baked mackerel with preserved lemon salsa verde (p49). Café Clock preserves its own capers when they come into season in September, but you can get them easily in any supermarket.

1   Toss the rocket, orange, avocado or fennel and capers together in a large bowl

2   Drizzle with argan oil and serve immediately

2 large, double-handfuls rocket, watercress or other robust salad leaves, washed and dried
1 orange, peeled and segmented
1 thinly shaved fennel bulb OR avocado, halved then sliced
2 tbsp capers, rinsed and dried
1–2 tbsp argan oil
salt and peper

Tomato and preserved lemon salad
(serves 4) (V)

This is a nice take on the more traditional tomato salad. It's also incredibly good stirred into a bowl of pasta (chop the tomatoes into dice if you are doing it this way).

1 Toss the ingredients together in a large bowl
2 Toast some bread or *khobz* and pile the tomato mix on top for a quick, Morocco-inspired version of the Italian bruschetta

3 large ripe tomatoes, cut into eighths
¼ preserved lemon (rind only), rinsed and thinly sliced
1 garlic clove, crushed
1 tbsp capers (optional)
large handful parsley, roughly chopped
1 tbsp olive oil
1 tsp salt

Oven-dried tomato and goat's cheese salad
(serves 4) (V)

In Morocco excess tomatoes are usually dried on the rooftops, but these are a good alternative if you don't have an abundance of sunshine. If you've got a day at home, it's worth taking the time to make them, but you do need to be around to keep an eye on them.

20–30 cherry tomatoes, halved
5 cloves garlic, minced
½ preserved lemon, flesh discarded, rinse peel and finely slice
5 tbsp olive oil
200 g goat's cheese or feta, cubed
2 tbsp pine nuts, toasted until golden
2 tbsp mint leaves
1 tbsp olive oil
sea salt

For the dried tomatoes

1 Preheat the oven to 100°C
2 In a bowl mix together the garlic, oil, lemon peel and salt, and toss with the tomatoes
3 Arrange the tomatoes on a baking tray, cut side up
4 Drizzle any remaining garlic and lemon mixture over the top
5 Place on a lower rack of the oven and bake for 3 hours until dried, but still moist
6 Leave to cool

To assemble the salad

1 Scatter the cheese over the top of the tomatoes (if you're using a log-shaped goat's cheese, cut into rounds, place on top of the tomatoes and grill to brown)
2 Sprinkle with pine nuts and mint leaves
3 Drizzle with olive oil and serve

Charmoula potato salad (serves 4) (V)

Tariq made this dish for the Clock's opening party and it's been a favourite ever since

1   Cook the potatoes in a pan of boiling water until tender, drain and leave to cool

2   Combine the charmoula and the olive oil, or mayonnaise, in a bowl

3   Toss through the potatoes, season with salt and pepper and garnish with parsley

1 kg potatoes, rinsed and diced

4 tbsp green or red charmoula (p147)

4 tbsp olive oil or mayonnaise

1 tbsp parsley, roughly chopped

salt and pepper

Harissa roast potatoes (serves 4) (V)

1   Preheat oven to 200°C

2   Toss the potatoes in the oil and harissa with a good pinch of salt and pepper

3   Bake for 45 minutes, tossing now and then, until brown and crunchy. With a dollop of saffron yogurt (p150) it's a great alternative to fries and mayo

1 kg potatoes, cut into thin wedges

2 tbsp harissa (wet or dry)

4 tbsp olive oil

salt and pepper

snacks

If Morocco doesn't have its own name for lots of little dishes – like tapas in Spain or mezze in Greece and Turkey – it should have, because it does snacking well. These dishes work equally well hot or cold, and most can be made at least a day in advance.

Although the Clock doesn't serve alcohol (it's prohibited within much of the medina), I'd recommend an ice-cold Moroccan gris (very pale rosé wine) from Meknes, a crisp Spanish fino or manzanilla, or even a glass of champagne.

Crispy fried sardines in ras al hanout (serves 4)

In Fez I always pick up supplies of ras al hanout – the legendary spice-trader's mix – from my pal Abdou deep in the medina. His mix is a fiery orange colour, as opposed to the dull brown of more industrial mixes, and he closely guards the secret blend of more than 49 different spices which, depending on how they are mixed – and his mood – double as magic spells for just about anything.

12–15 butterflied, fresh sardines or anchovies

1 tbsp flour

3 tbsp ras al hanout

1 tsp rose-petal infused salt (see p146)

1   Mix together the flour, ras al hanout and salt and dredge the sardines or anchovies in it until well covered

2   Heat vegetable oil in a shallow frying pan until smoking hot

3   Add the sardines skin side down and fry for about 30 seconds. Flip over with tongs and do the other side for about 30 seconds, until both sides are crunchy and golden

4   Drain on kitchen paper and serve immediately with a dollop of harissa mayo (p150) if you want to spice it up a bit

Charmoula olives (serves 4) (V)

The Clock uses its red charmoula mix for this as the sweetness of the paprika contrasts wonderfully with the bitter, bright, green Moroccan olives sold in the medina.

100 g un-pitted, green olives

4 tbsp red charmoula

1 preserved lemon

1   Remove the flesh from the lemon and discard it. Rinse the peel and cut into thin strips

2   Combine the olives and the lemon peel with the charmoula

3   Cover and leave to marinate in the fridge for at least 24 hours (these will last a couple of weeks if kept covered and chilled)

Quail's eggs, Clock-style (serves 4) (V)

There's something so simple and elegant about a dish of boiled eggs served with a choice of herbs and spices for sprinkling. We always use quail's eggs since they look so pretty, but you could also use fresh hen's eggs

12 quail's eggs
1 tsp sea salt
1 tsp cumin
1 tsp ras al hanout
1 tsp dry harissa (or a mix of paprika and chilli powder)

1   Soak the eggs in warm water for a few minutes and wipe clean, then add to a bowl of half vinegar half water to make them easy to peel

2   Bring a large pan of water to a rolling boil, gently add the eggs using a large serving spoon and boil for two and a half minutes (the yolk will be soft but not runny)

3   Remove the eggs and plunge into cool water to stop the cooking

4   Serve with small dishes of spices for dipping on the side

Goat's cheese in mint leaves (serves 4) (V)

The first time Tariq took me to visit Fatima (the lady who supplies the Clock with cheese) and her husband in the middle Atlas she made us a wonderful appetiser of goat's cheese and figs that we ate washed down with lots of mint tea. I think it would go just as well with a glass of fruity red wine.

200 g fresh goat's cheese or ricotta, mashed with a fork

1 tbsp honey

several large mint leaves

10 figs

1   Whisk together the goat's cheese and honey until you get a smooth, thick paste

2   Using a teaspoon put a small dollop of the paste in the centre of a mint leaf and wrap it up

3   Cut the figs in half and skewer it together with a mint and cheese parcel with a toothpick

Atlas almonds (serves 4) (V)

These make a quick nibble for drinks before dinner, and they are infinitely more exciting than a bag of peanuts.

100 g blanched almonds (if in their skins, boil for 60 seconds then the skin will slip off)

3 tbsp butter or olive oil

1 tbsp paprika

1 tbsp cinnamon

1 tbsp ground ginger

1 tsp cayenne pepper

1 tbsp brown sugar

1   Melt the butter in a wide frying pan until it foams

2   Add the spices and cook over a gentle heat until they begin to smell aromatic

3   Add the almonds and toss well

4   Leave to cool before serving

Moroccan wraps

Traditionally, *trid* is used in two ways: either like pasta, to form the base of stewy dishes like *r'fisa*, or more like a wrap as is typical in Marrakech, which is the way I prefer it. Either way, it's always soft and used for savoury dishes as opposed to warka, a similar gossamer-thin dough, which is generally used for sweet dishes and is crisp.

There is a recipe for *trid* on pp138–9, but the following is a cheat's version, which is a bit more manageable in a modern kitchen. I've used fish as the main ingredient for these fillings, but it works equally well with chicken, beef or lamb.

Spiced flatbread

1. Mix the dry ingredients, gradually adding the water and kneading until you have a soft, pliable dough (or use a food processor with a dough hook)
2. Shape the dough into a sausage shape and cut into 12–15 equal pieces
3. Flatten each out and roll out to form a round disc approx 1 mm thick
4. Meanwhile, heat a heavy frying pan and cook the flatbreads for about a minute on each side or until they are lightly golden with brown spots
5. Stack and wrap in foil to be reheated later on

500 g strong, white flour
1 tsp ground cumin
1 tsp ground coriander
1 tsp ground cinnamon
2 tsp ras al hanout
2 tsp salt
300–400 ml luke-warm water

Recipes for a range of fillings are given over the page. Allow 2 or 3 wraps per person and place a little of each filling in the centre of the flatbread, before rolling up and serving.

Harissa pickled onions

1 Place vinegar, lime juice and salt in a pan and gently heat until the salt dissolves

2 Pour over the raw onions, harissa and chillies and let stand at room temperature for 2–3 hours

3 Place in a glass jar and chill (these onions will keep refrigerated for about 2 weeks)

2 small red onions, halved then sliced

1 tsp harissa

1–2 red chillies

4 tbsp sherry vinegar

2 limes, juiced

1 tbsp salt

Charmoula fish

1 Slice the fish into fingers and marinate in the charmoula for 5–6 hours in the fridge

2 When ready to cook remove from the marinade and dredge in flour

3 Heat a shallow pan with oil and fry the fish fingers until golden (about 2 minutes either side)

4 Drain on kitchen paper and serve immediately

1 kg white fish fillets (haddock, cod, hake, pollack – any firm white fish will do)

4 tbsp red charmoula (see p. 147)

4 tbsp flour, seasoned with salt and pepper

oil for frying

Herbed goat's cheese

1 Mix the ingredients together in a bowl

2 Keep chilled until ready to serve

200 g fresh goat's cheese, mashed (or substitute ricotta and feta, mixed)

1 tbsp fresh coriander, finely chopped

1 tbsp fresh mint, finely chopped

1 tsp cumin

Tomato-lemon salsa

1 Combine all the ingredients together

2 Keep chilled until ready to serve

500 g fresh, diced tomatoes

1 preserved lemon, remove flesh and discard, rinse rind and finely dice

1 hot green chilli, sliced

4 garlic cloves, crushed

1 large sweet onion, diced

1 handful fresh coriander, roughly chopped

juice of 1–2 limes

pinch salt

cakes, pastries and desserts

Café Clock was always conceived as a place to feed the mind and soul as well as the body. On any given day you can learn Darija (the Moroccan Arabic dialect), calligraphy, yoga or belly-dancing, but it's also become an unofficial community centre for Fez's sociable young Moroccans, and expats. If you don't know where to find someone or something, it's as good a place as any to start: a modern-day *fondouk* (a traditional Moroccan coaching inn) if you like, where information is traded, friendships formed, and tales of life in the medina exchanged.

If you can do it over a glass of mint tea, or a *nousnous* (a strong espresso with a shot of hot milk) and a cake, then so much the better.

Chocolate brownies with cardamom and crystallised rose petals (makes 16–20)

These brownies are particularly festive and evocative of the smell of spice markets and the souks. I like to serve them warm with a dollop of crème fraîche or vanilla ice-cream.

1   Preheat the oven to 180°C and grease a baking tray (20 cm x 30 cm)

2   Cream together the butter and white and brown sugar until light and fluffy, and whisk in the egg

3   Melt the chocolate in a glass bowl over a pan of water, stir into the egg and butter cream, and add the cardamom

4   Fold in the sifted flour, baking powder, salt and grated apples and pour into the baking tray

5   Bake on the middle shelf of the oven for 50 minutes (insert a toothpick into the centre – if it comes out clean, it is done), cool in the baking tray

For the icing

1   Melt the chocolate and butter together in a glass bowl over a pan of hot water

2   Pour over the top of the cake when cooled, and scatter with pistachio nuts

3   Cut into squares and top each with a crystallised rose petal

225 g unsalted butter, softened

125 g white sugar

75 g brown sugar

1 egg

100 g dark chocolate

200 g plain white flour

1 sachet (16 g) or 1 heaped tbsp baking powder

½ tsp salt

3 apples, grated

10 cardamom pods, husks removed, seeds crushed in a pestle and mortar (or 1 tsp ground cardamom)

butter for greasing

For the icing

100 g dark chocolate

50 g butter

2 tbsp pistachio nuts, husks removed, roughly chopped

16–20 crystallised rose petals (see p152)

Behla (sesame shortcake) (makes 20)

Behla is the oldest *ghriba* (biscuit) in Fez and comes from a word meaning 'stupid girl'. Local lore has it that at some point back in time, an absent-minded kitchen girl forgot to add eggs to the mixture – with, it turned out, delicious results. You need to leave it overnight to prove, but the wait is worth it for cookies that dissolve like magic the minute they hit your tongue.

1 Mix all of the ingredients together with an electric mixer (it should form a smooth, very slightly moist dough, but should not be sticky)

2 Cover in clingfilm and leave overnight in the fridge

3 The next day preheat the oven to 180°C

4 Return the dough to the mixer, add the baking powder and mix again

5 Knead until smooth, then roll the dough out to ½ cm thick

6 Cut into rounds with a cookie cutter and bake for 20 minutes or until golden

7 Leave to cool on a wire rack and serve with a hot, strong shot of espresso

500 g plain flour

100 g icing sugar

3 heaped tbsp sesame seeds, toasted and pounded in a pestle and mortar, or ground in a coffee grinder

1 tbsp anis seeds, toasted and pounded in a pestle and mortar, or ground in a coffee grinder

½ tsp cinnamon

75 g butter, melted

75 g vegetable oil

pinch salt

1 sachet (16 g) or 1 heaped tbsp baking powder

Cinnamon spiced banana bread with candied lemon frosting (makes 1 medium sized loaf)

An ideal way to use up overripe, leftover bananas. The mushier they are, the better the bread.

1 Pre-heat oven to 180°C

2 Mix all of the ingredients together except the dates (use an electric whisk if you prefer) and when well combined, fold in the dates

3 Spoon the batter mixture into a 1 kg non-stick loaf tin, spread it out evenly and bake for 1½ hours. Stick a toothpick into the centre – if it emerges clean it's done

4 Cool on a wire rack, frost and serve

To make the frosting

1 Combine all the ingredients except the whole slices of candied lemon together in a food processor or blender. Spread over the top of the cooled cake

2 Decorate with preserved lemon slices

225 g self-raising flour

100 g butter

150 g caster sugar

450 g soft bananas, peeled and mashed

175 g chopped dates

2 eggs

1 tsp ground cinnamon

½ tsp salt

For the frosting

200 g cream cheese

110 g icing sugar

1 tbsp lemon juice

1 tbsp candied lemons cut into fine slivers, plus several thin slices of whole candied lemon

Date petits four (makes 12)

Tariq's beautiful stuffed dates are served at the Clock as petits four with coffee, in keeping with a tradition that ensures your guests leave with something sweet in their mouths, stomachs and souls to remember you by. Nothing could be more important to the Moroccan host.

1 Wipe the dates with orange blossom water to clean

2 Mix together the cheese, half the crushed walnuts, cardamom and honey, stuff 4 dates with the mixture and garnish with a whole walnut and a mint leaf

3 Knead together the marzipan, pistachio nuts and orange flower essence, and stuff 4 dates with the mixture – garnish each with 3 toasted almonds

4 Stir the crystallised ginger, the remainder of the crushed walnuts and the chopped almonds into half the melted chocolate, reserving a few pieces of ginger for decoration, stuff the dates with the chocolate mixture, then dip in the remaining melted chocolate, stud with a couple of pieces of reserved ginger and chill

12 large medjool dates, split open down one side and pit removed

2 tbsp orange blossom water

1 tbsp crystallised ginger, finely diced

1 tbsp almonds, finely chopped

2 tbsp walnuts, crushed

180 g dark chocolate, melted

2 tbsp mascarpone

2 cardamom pods, husks removed, seeds crushed

1 tbsp honey

4 mint leaves

4 walnuts, whole

2 tbsp marzipan

1 tbsp pistachio nuts, crushed

3 drops orange-flower essence

12 toasted almonds

Coconut ghriba (Moroccan macaroons) (makes 20)

One of Morocco's favourite sweetmeats, you'll see these sold from street carts all over the medina. They are completely addictive.

250 g desiccated coconut
100 g fine semolina
125 g sugar
2 eggs
pinch salt
zest of 1 orange or lemon
40 g each butter (melted) and vegetable oil
1 tsp baking powder
1 tbsp orange-blossom water

1 Preheat oven to 180°C

2 Beat together the eggs and sugar in a pan over a very low heat (the eggs shouldn't cook, but the sugar should dissolve), stir in the salt and zest

3 Stir in the melted butter and oil, and fold in the semolina, baking powder and coconut. Chill for 15–20 minutes

4 Moisten palms with orange blossom water and roll the dough into small balls, dip one side in icing sugar, flatten slightly and bake for 20 minutes

5 Turn on to wire rack to cool

Date and orange cheesecake

The date and orange cheesecake is as much a Clock classic as the camel burger.

1   Preheat the oven to 200°C

2   Line a 22 cm cake tin with a removable base with greaseproof paper

3   Using an electric mixer or wooden spoon blend the biscuits with the butter to achieve a fine crumb, press into the cake tin and bake for 8 minutes

4   Remove the base from the oven and allow to cool slightly

5   Cream together the cheese, cream, eggs, sugar and salt, stir in the dates and orange zest and pour on top of the biscuit base

6   Bake in a bain-marie for 30 minutes

7   Leave to cool for at least an hour before removing it from the tin

250 g oat or digestive biscuits, crushed
100 g butter, melted
1 kg mascarpone cheese
180 g sugar
250 ml fresh cream
5 eggs
½ tsp salt
zest of 5 oranges
10 dates, cut into slivers

Variation – chocolate

Once the biscuit base has cooked and cooled, spread over 100 g melted dark chocolate. Stir 1 tbsp each of dark, milk and white chocolate chips into the cheese mix instead of the orange zest and dates and bake as normal.

Variation – lemon and ginger

Substitute lemon zest and crystallised ginger for the orange zest and dates, and bake as normal.

Honey souk tarte tatin

About two hundred metres from the Clock is the medina's honey souk. Here you will find Hicham Nafis, who collects speciality honey from all over Morocco, including honey from wild bees. The location of the hives themselves remains a closely guarded secret, but for a rare peek at this gastronomic treat step inside: the bright, turquoise-painted room is filled with blue pails of thick, viscous liquids ranging from milky pale to almost black. It's worth passing by for a tasting and the staff at the Clock can often be found there buying small chunks of fresh honeycomb to snack on between shifts.

250 g shop-bought puff pastry, thawed

2 Granny Smith apples, peeled, cored and cut into eighths (keep them in a bowl of cold water until ready to use to stop them from going brown)

2 tbsp butter

3 tbsp herb or flower honey, such as rosemary or lavender

2 cinnamon sticks

1 Preheat the oven to 180°C

2 Melt the butter in a saucepan, add the cinnamon sticks and the honey. When foaming add the apples

3 Cook for 7–8 minutes until the apples are tender, but not mushy

4 Spread the apple mixture over a shallow, buttered baking dish and press the pastry into the top

5 Glaze with melted butter, and bake for 15 minutes or until the pastry is golden

6 Allow to cool a little before turning out on to a plate, serve while still warm with a dollop of whipped cream or thick, Greek yoghurt

Orange cream tart (makes one large tart to serve 10, or 12 small tarts)

1   Add 110 g sugar and butter to the orange juice and bring to the boil

2   Whisk together the egg yolks and whole eggs with 110 g sugar, a pinch of salt, cornflour and orange zest and fold into the still bubbling juice

3   Turn the heat off and whisk well to ensure the custard cooks, but the eggs don't coagulate, sieve to get a smooth cream, whip once more with an electric mixer if you have one, cover and chill well

4   Spoon into individual pie shells just before serving to keep the crust crisp

To make the pie crust

1   Preheat oven to 200°C

2   Rub together the flour and butter to form a crumb, add the rest of the ingredients and mix in an electric food mixer for 30 seconds (it should look like a shortbread dough), chill for 1 hour

3   Press into pastry shells and prick with a fork

4   Bake for 10–15 minutes

600 ml freshly squeezed orange juice
8 egg yolks
4 whole eggs
350 g butter
220 g sugar
2 tbsp cornflour
zest of 2 oranges
pinch salt

For the pie crust
500 g plain flour
250 g butter
200 g sugar
1 tsp vanilla essence
2 whole eggs
pinch sea salt

Lemon cream tart (makes one large tart to serve 10, or 12 small tarts)

1 Add 180 g sugar and butter to the lemon juice and bring to the boil

2 Whisk together the egg yolks and eggs with 180 g sugar, a pinch of salt, the cornflour and lemon zest and fold into the still bubbling juice

3 Turn the heat off and whisk well to ensure the custard cooks but the eggs don't coagulate, pass through a sieve to get a smooth cream, whip once more with an electric mixer if you have one, cover and chill well

4 Spoon into individual pie shells just before serving to keep the crust crisp

To make the pie crust

1 Preheat oven to 200°C

2 Rub together the flour and butter to form a crumb, add the rest of the ingredients and mix in an electric food mixer for 30 seconds (it should look like a shortbread dough), chill for 1 hour

3 Press into pastry shells and prick with a fork

4 Bake for 10–15 minutes

600 ml freshly squeezed lemon juice
8 egg yolks
4 whole eggs
350 g butter
360 g sugar
2 tbsp cornflour
zest of 2 lemons
pinch salt

For the pie crust
500 g plain flour
250 g butter
200 g sugar
1 tsp vanilla essence
2 whole eggs
pinch sea salt

Moulay Idriss briouat (makes 30)

Moulay Idriss was the founder of the sacred city about 20 minutes north of Meknes that bears his name. For Moroccan Muslims it is second only to Mecca as a pilgrimage site. Until quite recently, it was forbidden for non-Muslims to stay in the town of Moulay Idriss and though these rules have relaxed considerably it still exudes a deeply spiritual feel that can't help but overtake you when you arrive.

The town is also known for its food. The olive oil produced here is considered to be the best in Morocco, the country's finest vineyards are less than an hour away, and the women are known for the lightness of their pastries, which convey a lightness of heart to the eater. The following was taught to me by a woman called Saïda (meaning 'happy' in Darija).

200 g toasted peanuts, skins removed (substitute almonds or pistachios if you prefer, or use a mix of all three)

25 g sugar

2 tsp ground cinnamon

2 tbsp orange blossom water

2 tbsp vegetable oil

4 warka (or filo) sheets

1 tbsp butter, melted

4 tbsp honey, warmed

vegetable oil for deep frying

1   Grind the peanuts using an electric spice grinder, or with a pestle and mortar, until you get a fairly fine crumb (like couscous, as they would say in Morocco)

2   Add the rest of the ingredients and mix well with the hands to make a moist paste (add a little more oil if needed)

3   Form into small, plum-shaped balls with your hands

4   Cut the warka into squares and wrap around the nut mix (you can form them into triangles, squares or roll into cigar-shapes) sealing them with a slick of butter

5   Fill a saucepan with vegetable oil up to about 2 inches, and heat to smoking hot

6   Deep fry the briouat, several at a time, until golden, then plunge into a bowl of warmed honey

7   Immediately remove from the honey and leave to cool on a plate lined with baking paper

Orange and cinnamon salad (serves 4)

The easiest dessert in the world, one of the prettiest and delightfully light after a heavy meal.

1   Toss together and serve

3 good oranges (blood oranges are the best for this), peeled, pith removed and sliced (or segmented)
3 tbsp good honey
2 tbsp orange blossom water
150 g pistachios
1 tsp cinnamon

Poached peaches with yoghurt, candied walnuts and honey

Morocco's stone fruit are exceptional and abundant during their short season. This light, summery desert will work well with any of them.

1   Dissolve the sugar in the water over a medium heat
2   Add the whole peaches and poach in the liquid for 15 minutes, leave to cool in the syrup
3   Peel the peaches, cut in half and serve with a dollop of Greek yoghurt and sprinkle with candied walnuts

100 g sugar
500 ml water
4 peaches
2 tbsp walnuts
1 tbsp butter
1 tbsp honey
100 ml Greek yoghurt

To make the walnuts
1   Melt the butter and sugar in a frying pan
2   When foaming add the walnuts and gently fry until the butter has evaporated and stuck to the nuts
3   Cool on a sheet of baking paper before serving

Pomegranate meringues (serves 4)

This is a fabulous-looking dish that you can either serve individually, or pile into a heap to make pavlova. It's sold at the Clock during pomegranate season from October to November. You could of course adapt to suit any fruit or berries that are in season.

For the pomegranate syrup
400 ml pomegranate juice
250 g caster sugar
1 tsp lemon juice
2 sticks cinnamon
3 star anise

For the meringues
3 large eggs, separated
150 g caster sugar

To assemble the meringues
seeds of one pomegranate
200 g mascarpone cheese
200 ml whipping cream

1   In a saucepan, combine pomegranate juice, sugar and lemon juice over medium heat until the sugar has completely dissolved

2   Add the spices and continue to cook over medium-high heat for 20–25 minutes, or until juice is the consistency of syrup.

3   Remove from heat, strain to remove the spices and allow to cool

4   Store in airtight container in the refrigerator for up to two weeks

To make the meringues

1   Preheat oven to 150°C

2   Whisk the egg whites together on a slow speed for 2–3 minutes or until foamy

3   Turn up to a medium speed and continue whisking for 1 minute, then turn up to high speed and whisk until soft peaks start to form

4   Whisk in the sugar on a high speed, but stop the minute a shiny, thick whipped cream starts to form

5   Spoon (using a clean, dry stainless steel spoon) or pipe onto a tray lined with baking paper

6   Turn the oven down to 140°C and bake for 1½ hours

7   Turn off the oven and allow the meringues to cool inside it or leave overnight so that they properly dry out

To assemble the meringues

1   Combine the mascarpone cheese with 4–5 tbsp pomegranate syrup

2   Spread one flat side of meringue with the cheese mix, sprinkle with pomegranate seeds and sandwich together with another meringue

3   Serve with a dollop of fresh cream and more pomegranate seeds

Rosewater pannacotta (serves 4)

A glass of almond milk spiked with rosewater is a traditional welcome in many Moroccan homes, and so inspired this gorgeous pannacotta as the sweetest way to say dinner's over.

375 ml cream
125 ml milk
1 tsp rose essence
60 g caster sugar
1 vanilla pod
1½ gelatine sheets
1 candied lemon
4 crystallised rose petals
1 tbsp pistachio nuts, crushed

1   Combine the cream, milk, rose essence and sugar together in a saucepan; slit the vanilla pod and scrape the seeds into the milk mix; add the vanilla pod itself and bring to a gentle simmer over a low heat

2   Strain into a mixing bowl and discard the vanilla pod

3   Soak the gelatine sheets in a little cold water for 2 minutes to soften, squeeze out the excess moisture and whisk into the cream while still warm, ensuring the gelatine completely dissolves

4   Strain into 4 small, 100 ml dariole moulds, or ramekins

5   Set overnight in the fridge

6   When ready to serve, gently run a small knife around the inside of the moulds so the pannacotta comes away from the edge and gently tap on to serving plates

7   Top with a thin slice of candied lemon, a rose petal and a sprinkle of crushed pistachio nuts

breads

The staff of the Clock kitchen have always relied on their eyes and instincts when it comes to cooking. In traditional Moroccan kitchens you'll never see measuring cups, spoons or even a set of scales and although measurements are included here, it is instinct that is key when it comes to your daily bread.

Once you've baked bread the Moroccan way – meaning wet and messy – you'll never look back. The dough is assembled in a shallow terracotta dish (traditionally unglazed, but more usually glazed these days) called a *gsaa*. Once the flour, salt and water is combined the dough is mixed around with the hands, stretched and folded over and over again until plump and elastic, left to rise twice and then carried away to the *ferran* (community bakers). In Morocco people are happy to pick up bread from a neighbour and drop it off at the *ferran* if they happen to be passing, a task often picked up by young children. It has always amazed me how the bakers know whose bread belongs to whom, and it always comes back safe and sound, warm and fragrant a half-hour later. There are infinite different styles, ranging from day-to-day *khobz*, served with just about anything, to the complicated knots and twists of the spectacular *turban du juge*, which I have to confess I'm not expecting to master any time soon.

Bread is sacred in Morocco and even at the Clock is rarely thrown away. One day while learning to make *melawi* – a stuffed bread that might be described as a kind of Moroccan pizza – I was told about a slave who was imprisoned for all eternity in the moon because she defiled a loaf. It serves as a cautionary tale to all: if you see a piece on the ground you should pick it up, kiss it and remove it from harm's way (hence the proliferation of old loaves crammed between the crevices of these ancient medina houses) before carrying on your way.

Harsha (makes 6 individual sized breads)

I like this crumbly bread all on its own or hot and spread with butter (it's especially popular with children as a teatime snack). But it's also great with hummus or the various salads included in this book.

250g coarse semolina plus extra for dusting

100g fine semolina

100g butter, melted

1 sachet (9g) baking powder

2tsp sugar

pinch salt

500ml milk

1   Rub all of the ingredients together to form a fine breadcrumb that looks like couscous, chill

2   When you are ready to use it, mix with just enough milk to bind the dough together, shape into a flat patty and dust with coarse semolina

3   Cook in a heavy pan over a medium heat for 10 mins, flip and cook on the other side

4   Serve hot

Khobz (makes 6 individual sized breads)

Arabic *khobz* is the daily bread of the nation, and indeed of the Café Clock. The use of two types of semolina flour in this recipe gives the bread its distinctive texture and character, but you could just use strong, plain flour at home, or experiment with spelt, kamut or Saracen (buckwheat) flours.

300 g strong, white flour (or barley flour, if you can get it)

100 g fine semolina flour

100 g coarse semolina flour

1 tbsp fresh, crumbled yeast or 1 sachet dried yeast

1 tsp sea salt

320–350 g warm water for mixing (weighed water rather than measured in a jug is much more accurate; depending on how coarse the flour is, you may need a little extra)

1 Mix together the flours and salt in a shallow mixing bowl. Dig a well in the centre, add the yeast and top off with a splash of warm water. Leave it to rest for a couple of minutes to allow the yeast to start working

2 Adding a small amount of water at a time, mix well with your hands. It will get sticky and messy, but persevere. After 10 minutes or so of kneading, a smooth and elastic dough will start to form (do not be tempted to add more flour, it will change the consistency of your bread)

3 Tip the dough on to a very lightly floured surface. Flour your hands and continue to knead for another 5 minutes or so until the dough is soft and plump-looking (it should spring back into place when you press it with your index finger)

4 Return to a lightly floured bowl, cover with a tea towel and leave it to rise for at least an hour

5 Roll the dough into a sausage shape and divide into six sections, knead each into a flat round disk and place on a baking tray lined with paper; cover with a tea towel and leave to rise another hour

6 Preheat oven to 180°C

7 Bake the rolls for 20 minutes (when ready, they should sound hollow when you tap them)

8 Turn on to a wire rack and leave to cool.

To make in a food processor

If you have a food mixer with a dough hook, mix all of the ingredients together on the lowest setting and slowly pour in the rest of the water as it mixes. After 2–3 minutes set the speed a little higher and continue to mix for 7–8 minutes until a smooth, elastic dough forms. Remove from the mixer and continue as above from 3.

Goat's cheese, oregano and preserved lemon khobz (makes 6 individual sized breads)

1 At stage 2 of the dough-making process add the dried oregano and preserved lemon rind (well rinsed)

2 At stage 5 push the goat's cheese into the dough

3 Shape the dough into rolls as before, brush with argan or olive oil over the top and bake for 20 minutes

4 Turn on to a wire rack to cool.

Additional ingredients

2 tbsp dried oregano

2 tbsp chopped preserved lemon rind

100 g hard goat's cheese or feta, in 2 cm dice

argan or olive oil

Fennel seed khobz (makes 6 individual sized breads)

1 At stage 2 of the dough-making process add the toasted fennel seeds

2 Shape the dough into rolls as before, brush with argan or olive oil over the top, sprinkle with the raw fennel seeds and sea salt, and bake for 20 minutes

4 Turn on to a wire rack to cool.

Additional ingredients

2 tbsp fennel seeds, divided (toast one half and crush in a pestle and mortar, keep the other half raw)

argan or olive oil

sea salt

Spice trader's flatbread

I like this flatbread hot from the oven all on its own, but it also works well with a mild cheese like mozzarella, which picks up the flavours nicely. Scatter slices of the cheese over the flatbread halfway through cooking and cook through until the cheese is bubbling and lightly golden.

1 batch khobz (see p134)

2 tbsp ras al hanout

4 tbsp argan oil (alternatively use olive oil)

2 balls mozzarella (optional), sliced

1. Split the khobz into 6 sections, but don't bake
2. Mix together the ras al hanout (if you can't get ras al hanout use a mix of cumin, paprika, cinnamon and coriander) and argan oil
3. Preheat the oven to 180°C
4. Roll out the dough sections until approx 1 mm thick
5. Generously brush the spice mix over the top, then fold once, brush again with the spice mix and fold again
6. Roll out to approx 1 mm thick, brush one final time with the spice mix and bake on the middle shelf until golden (approx 20 minutes)

Variation

This also works well substituting *za'atar* (p146) for ras al hanout.

Stuffed melawi

You see *melawi* at bread stalls all over Morocco. It's a layered flatbread folded into squares and brushed with lashings of butter. At its most delicious it becomes a kind of Moroccan pizza, stuffed with meat or savoury onions. In Marrakech they call it *r'ghaif* and it can be very oily. I prefer the slightly healthier Fassi version, which is cooked on a hot aluminium pan or, in this case, in the oven.

1 Combine the flour, salt and yeast in a shallow bowl, and sift through your fingers to aerate it a little

2 Slowly add warm water, kneading well. As the dough begins to form add a splash more water to the base of your bowl

3 Stretch the dough out so that it covers the water and fold it back into shape, splashing or dribbling the water into the layers. Repeat several times until the water is worked into the dough and it starts to feel silky

4 Leave to prove for 20 minutes

To make the stuffing mix

1 Combine all the ingredients (except for the fresh parsley and coriander) in a pan, bring to a boil and simmer gently for 30 minutes until thick and glossy

2 Leave to cool slightly before folding in the fresh herbs

To assemble the melawi

1 Roll out the dough sections until approx 1 mm thick

2 Spread the stuffing mix over the top, fold once, add more stuffing mix and fold again

3 Roll out to approx 1 mm thick, brush the top with argan (or olive) oil and bake on the middle shelf until golden (approx 20 minutes)

400 g plain flour

1 tsp salt

1 tsp dried yeast

320–350 g warm water for mixing (weighed water rather than measured in a jug is much more accurate; depending on how coarse the flour is, you may need a little extra)

For the stuffing

1 onion, finely diced

50 g minced beef or lamb (optional)

1 tbsp olive oil

2 tsp dried oregano

1 tsp paprika

1 tsp cumin

½ tsp cayenne pepper

½ tsp salt

1 tbsp fresh coriander, chopped

1 tbsp fresh parsley, chopped

Trid (makes 12 sheets of trid)

Nothing warms my heart more than visiting the women *trid* bakers at the food market in r'Cif. I remember the first time I went to Fez seeing them spinning wafer-thin discs of dough like Italian pizza boys, but rather than catching the dough, they would lay it over the surface of a giant, blackened, terracotta 'egg'. It was one of the most intriguing things I had ever seen.

250g plain flour
1½tsp salt
150ml cold water
50ml olive oil
50ml vegetable oil

Staff at the Clock told me that most people wouldn't bother to make it at home these days – they'd buy it from the ladies in the medina. It is still possible to find the traditional *terraada* – a terracotta domed vessel that you place above a gas hob – and since the Clock kitchen tries to use as many traditional cooking tools as possible in its classes, I bought them one.

Should you be tempted to buy one, make sure you choose a *terraada* with no cracks. Oil it well with olive oil, rubbing well into the earthenware surface, and repeat over and over again until the oil stops soaking in and surface has a soft sheen. It's then ready to use. New, they cost about 50 dirham (€5), though cooks here would prefer to buy a second-hand one that has been oiled and seasoned already, proving it can stand up to the heat of the flame.

1. Pour flour and salt into a flat, glazed bowl – a tagine is perfect if you have it

2. Add the water very gradually and combine with the flour, stretching the dough out flat and folding it over itself to work in lots of air

3. It will be sticky at first but keep kneading for 5–10 minutes and a smooth, elastic dough will start to form

4. Roll it into a sausage shape, fold and repeat. Continue like this for another 10 minutes or so. The more you work the dough, the more elastic it will be

5. It is ready when it stretches easily without breaking and when it springs back into shape easily when you press it with a finger

6. Combine the olive and vegetable oils in an oblong dish, douse your hands in the oil and separate the dough into golf ball sized balls

7. Place them in the oil to rest for at least 30 minutes

8. Oil a marble surface or chopping board (wood is too absorbent) and place a ball of dough on it

9. Roll or flatten the dough out, flipping over from time to time, until you have a large, flat, almost translucent sheet

10. Carefully pick up the *trid* and transfer it to the *terraada*, once it has changed colour quickly rip it from the *terraada* and turn over (if you don't have one, use a very hot, cast-iron frying pan

11. Don't worry if it doesn't retain a perfectly round shape, it's the texture of this bread that makes it so good for mopping up juices, particularly in *r'fisa*

Pitta bread puff balls (makes 4 small pittas)

The Moroccan 'pitta' comes out at the start of the agricultural season, when farmers are out ploughing the fields and planting the seeds. On the first Saturday that the land once more becomes 'alive', children across all of rural Morocco are treated to a special pitta called *hagouz*, which is topped with peanuts, dates and raisins before it is baked.

200 g plain white flour

125 g fine semolina flour (or wholemeal, if preferred)

1 tbsp dried or fresh yeast

2 tsp salt

1½ tsp sugar

200 ml warm water

1   Mix the flours together, form a well in the centre of the flour and add the yeast, salt and sugar on top

2   Pour on a small amount of warm water to activate the yeast and leave for 1 minute

3   Gradually add more water and squelch the dough through your fingers to aerate it, drawing more flour in from the sides of the bowl as you do so, stretching the dough out flat and folding it over itself to work in lots of air (this is crucial if you want puffy pittas)

4   It will be sticky at first, but keep kneading for 5–10 minutes and a smooth, elastic dough will start to form

5   Roll it into a sausage shape, fold and repeat. Continue for another 10 minutes or so. The more you work the dough, the more elastic it will be

6   It is ready when it stretches easily without breaking and when you press your finger into the top of it, it comes back into shape quickly

7   Split the dough into four equal balls and oil them to prevent the surface from drying out, leave to rise for 20 minutes

8   Flatten the balls and roll out into 1 mm thick rounds

9   Heat a cast-iron frying pan wiped with a little bit of vegetable oil to prevent sticking

10. Add the pittas and cook over a gentle heat turning often so that they cook evenly but don't burn (approx 4 minutes) or until they puff up

pickles,
preserves,
condiments

The following recipes are all the things that make up the backbone of the Moroccan kitchen. Every household has them, stashed away in a pantry ready to add the richly complex flavours that turn Moroccan cooking into something extraordinary. Most are easy to make and worth the effort.

Za'atar

Ground dried herbs mixed with ground toasted sesame seeds. Variations of it appear across the whole of North Africa and the Middle East. It's great simply dipped with olive oil and warm bread, as a dry rub for meat, sprinkled over salads and dips such as hummus, or as an alternative topping for spice trader's flatbread (p136). Moroccan *za'atar* refers to thyme, marjoram and oregano. The Middle Eastern version converts this to a mix for dipping. This is my version, which combines the best of both worlds.

4 tbsp sesame seeds, toasted
2 tbsp dried thyme
2 tbsp dried marjoram
2 tbsp dried oregano
2 tbsp sumac
½ tsp salt

1   Grind together all ingredients using a hand blender

Infused salts

These are the easiest salts on earth to make, and work wonders with a simple piece of grilled chicken or fish. You make them all in exactly the same way: simply mix the ingredients together in a glass, airtight jar and let the flavours develop for one week before using. They also look really pretty on the table.

Rose petal salt

50 g sea salt
2 tbsp dried rose petals (if you can get dried petals from the Atlas mountains, all the better)

Orange and chilli salt

100 g sea salt
peel (avoid pith) of one orange (either use a zester or finely slice) and left on a piece of baking paper to dry for 24 hours before adding to the salt
2 dried red chillies, crumbled

Lemon and lavender salt

100 g sea salt
peel (avoid pith) of one lemon (either use a zester or finely slice) and left on a piece of baking paper to dry for 24 hours before adding to the salt
2 tsp dried lavender petals

Charmoula

Charmoula is Morocco's most important spice mix after ras al hanout. It's a tangy rather than spicy blend of fresh parsley and coriander, garlic, lemon juice and fire-red paprika and is most often seen in the excellent fish dishes of Essaouira. The Clock makes a red and a green version of it – the method is the same for both – and uses it to enliven any number of dishes.

It's also worth asking in medina spice stores for a dry version of charmoula that can be used as rub before barbecuing fish and meat.

1 Combine all the ingredients together in a bowl (or use a hand blender or food processor), cover and chill for at least 1 hour before using to let the flavours develop

Green charmoula

1 large handful fresh coriander, chopped (stalks removed)

1 large handful fresh parsley, chopped (stalks removed)

8 cloves garlic, crushed

2–3 hot green chillies, finely chopped

1 tsp sea salt

50 ml olive oil

50 ml lemon juice

Red charmoula

1 large handful fresh coriander, chopped (stalks removed)

1 large handful fresh parsley, chopped (stalks removed)

8 cloves garlic, crushed

1 tbsp bright red paprika

1 tsp cumin, ground

1 tsp black pepper, ground

1 tsp sea salt

50 ml olive oil

50 ml lemon juice

Harissa

Harissa is a Tunisian chilli sauce that has been enthusiastically adopted in Morocco and is sold either wet or dry. Wet it is tangy with a little sweetness and a fire-hot kick. Use sparingly.

Wet harissa (makes 500 ml)

1 Put everything through a blender and whizz until smoothish

2 Leave overnight to allow the flavours to develop, store in an airtight container and it's ready to use

500 g fresh hot chillies, seeds in

5 tbsp white wine vinegar

2 tbsp lemon juice

1 tsp salt

pinch sugar

Dry harissa

1 Mix together and store in an airtight container for sprinkling on *b'sarra* or for dipping grilled meats

2 tbsp bright red paprika

1 tbsp cayenne pepper

Three types of preserved lemons

Limon dduk (pronounced duck) are tiny, thin-skinned lemons that you often see in the medina and they make the best preserved lemons – so good you can snack on them alone, as you would olives or almonds. Unfortunately, *dduk* are not easy to get outside Morocco, but if you're in the US you might try using key limes. Otherwise the following will work well with any kind of lemon, providing it is unwaxed.

Traditional preserved lemons

1   Top and tail the lemons and cut into quarters without going right down to the bottom

2   Stuff the crosses with sea salt flakes

3   Squash down into a 1 litre glass jar with a rubber seal, top up so that the lemons are just covered with fresh lemon juice and water

4   Seal and store in a cool, dark place. They should be ready in about three weeks

Spiced lemons

1   Top and tail the lemons and cut into quarters without going right down to the bottom

2   Stuff the crosses with sea salt flakes and the spices (you can add anything you like except garlic, which will overpower the fruit)

3   Pack the lemons into a 1 litre glass jar with a rubber seal, top up so that the lemons are just covered with fresh lemon juice and water

4   Seal and store in a cool, dark place. Tip gently every couple of days to distribute the spices. They should be ready in about three weeks

Traditional

4 lemons

lemon juice of 2–3 lemons

enough sea salt flakes to cover

water

Spiced

4 lemons

lemon juice of 2–3 lemons

enough sea salt flakes to cover

2 tbsp whole black peppercorns

5 whole dried chillies

8 cardamom pods

water

Candied

4 lemons

750 g sugar

¾ litre water

Candied lemons

These lemons are Jewish in origin and aren't generally something you see in the preserves stalls of the medina, although you might see them in the Mellah (historically, the Jewish quarter).

1. Place whole lemons in a pan of water and bring to the boil, simmer for 3 minutes and leave to cool in the water, then cut into quarters without going all the way through

2. Boil the sugar and 1/3 litre water for 15 minutes, add the lemons and cook for 30 minutes on a gentle simmer until the skin is tender

3. Place the lemons in a sterilised glass jar, but continue cooking the syrup for a further 20 minutes on a very low heat

4. Cover the lemons with the sugar syrup and leave for 10 days before using

Fig and date chutney (makes 2 litres)

1 Combine all of the ingredients in a pan and cook for 1 hour over a medium heat until thick and glossy, stirring occasionally so it doesn't burn or stick to the bottom

2 Sterilise your jars by placing in boiling water, put the hot chutney in the jars and leave in the boiling water with the lids on for 2 minutes, this will seal them

3 Keep in a cool, dark place for at least 4 weeks before eating

2 kg fresh figs, quartered
225 g pitted dates, halved
1¼ litre red wine vinegar
500 g brown sugar
6 hot chillies, sliced
50 g fresh ginger, grated
2 tbsp paprika
1 tbsp mustard seeds
½ tbsp black pepper
2 tsp salt

Preserved lemon chutney (makes 1 litre)

1 Quarter the preserved lemons. Remove the flesh and discard, keeping the peel. Rinse the peel well in cold water and slice thinly.

2 Combine with the remainder of the ingredients in a pan and cook for 1 hour over a medium heat until thick and glossy, stirring occasionally so it doesn't burn or stick to the bottom

3 Sterilise your jars by placing in boiling water, put the hot chutney in the jars and leave in the boiling water with the lids on for 2 minutes, this will seal them

4 Keep in a cool, dark place for at least 4 weeks before eating

12 preserved lemons
250 g dates, pitted and quartered
25 g tamarind paste
6 cloves garlic, sliced
2 tbsp ginger, crated
1 tsp coriander seeds, crushed
½ tsp chilli flakes
½ tsp cayenne pepper
750 ml cider vinegar
250 ml lemon juice

Saffron yoghurt

1 Leave the saffron to infuse in the water for a minute or two, then stir into the Greek yoghurt

2 Cover and refrigerate for at least 30 minutes to let the flavours develop

25 g Greek yoghurt
1 tsp saffron threads, toasted and crumbled between the palms, then added to 1 scant tsp warm water

Harissa mayo

1 Combine the lot in a bowl. Cover and refrigerate for at least 30 minutes to let the flavours develop before serving

5 tsp good quality mayonnaise (or make your own)
½–1 tsp wet harissa (depending on how hot you like it)

Rose petal syrup (makes 200 ml)

Only use organic or home-grown rose petals (shop-bought ones are sprayed with all manner of nastiness).

1   Place the rose petals in the water, bring to a boil for 15 minutes, turn the heat off and leave to steep for 1 hour

2   Strain, discard the petals, add the lemon juice and sugar and simmer for 30 minutes

3   Mix the cornstarch with 1 tbsp cold water and add to the boiling rose petal juice, simmer for 5 minutes

4   Pour into a sterilised jar and cool. It is ready to use immediately

enough red rose petals to fill a one-litre jug
1 litre water
1 kg sugar
2 tbsp cornstarch
juice of 1 lemon

Crystallised rose petals (makes 24)

Make sure you use organic or home-grown rose petals to make these – those that have been sprayed with pesticides (as is the case in most commercial roses you can buy from florists) are not edible. They are super-easy to make. Make sure it is a dry day, or work in an air-conditioned room. Humidity will ruin the drying process.

24 organic or home-grown rose petals (you can use any colour)
1 egg white
1 tbsp water
2 tbsp caster sugar

1   Line a tray with baking paper

2   Dilute the egg white with the water

3   Using a small paintbrush paint each rose petal with the egg white solution so that it is well covered; sprinkle each side with sugar

4   Shake off the excess sugar and lay the rose petal on the baking paper

5   Leave in a cool, dry place for at least 8 hours moving from time to time so that they don't stick

6   Store in an airtight container (they will keep for up to a year)

Peach and apricot jam (makes 1½ litres)

Fruit, and stone fruit in particular, is extremely good in Morocco, reaching the medina at peak ripeness, so it's the perfect place for jam-making. The Clock makes various seasonal jams. My favourite is the apricot, but you could substitute pretty much any fruit that is in season.

1 kg fresh apricots
1 kg sugar
125 ml water
1 tbsp freshly squeezed lemon juice
1 tbsp orange-blossom water

1 Halve the apricots and remove the stone, add them to the water and bring to a boil

2 Simmer until the apricots are tender, then add the sugar

3 Skim off any foam that forms on the surface and continue to cook gently for 30 minutes or so, stirring frequently to stop it from burning

4 When the jam is good and thick test it by placing a small amount on a cold plate and place in the freezer for a couple of minutes. If it wrinkles when you nudge it, it is done. If it doesn't, you need to cook it for a little while longer

5 Stir in the lemon juice and orange-blossom water and pour into sterilised jars, cover and leave to cool. It is ready to use at any time

index

Acknowledgements

I'd like to thank Tahir Shah, who first told me to write about camel burgers. Mike Richardson for giving me the opportunity to create this book with him. Max, Souad and Tariq, as well as all the staff at Café Clock, too many to name, and without whom this book would have been impossible. Gail Leonard of Fez Food for showing me my way around a tangia. The various food vendors of the Fez medina who shared recipes, ideas and knowledge about Moroccan food and cooking. Julius Honnor for his generosity in providing fabulous photos, Claudia Roden for taking the time to look it over, Sally Davies for her invaluable last-minute proof-reading, and last and by no means least, my editor and publisher, Andrew Morris at 33books, who believed in us all and the project enough to take it on.

مقهى
الساعة

CafE
CLOCK

←